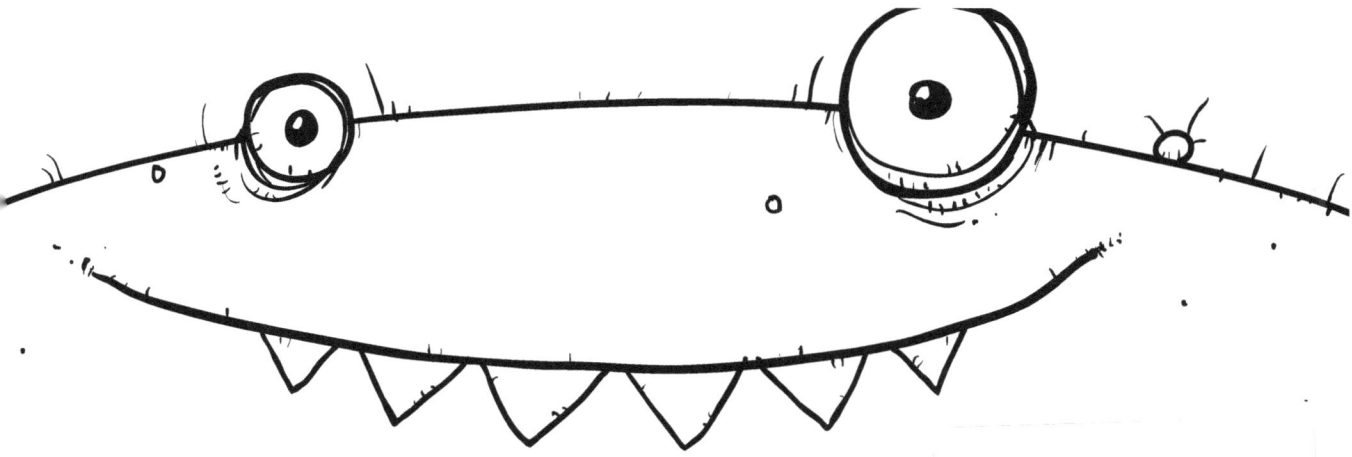

The Grownups' ABCs of Conflict Resolution | 2nd Edition

with illustrations by Dean Murray

TO: _____

FROM: _____

DATE: _____

"Pynchon provides women with what most dogs know; how to sniff out an asshole then take appropriate action, whatever action that might be. A must read for the timid girl/woman who needs to add boldness and audacity to her repertoire."

Ellen Snortland

Author of "Beauty Bites Beast," and "The Safety Godmother"; Pasadena Weekly columnist, Huffington Post and Ms. Magazine Blogger

———————

"After reading Victoria Pynchon's book-- I really now understand the meaning of We're Not Gonna Take It -- this book rocks!"

Jay Jay French

Twisted Sister

———————

"Victoria has approached this subject with a fresh eye, offering something for everyone. The result is an engaging, quintessential handbook and a must-have on the 'hows and whys' of conflict resolution. Best of all, she offers solutions. I highly recommend."

Cathy Scott

Author of "The Killing of Tupac Shakur", "The Murder of Biggie Smalls" and "Murder of a Mafia Daughter"

———————

"If you always wanted a raw, gutsy, no-holds-barred, emotionally wrenching, profoundly inspiring, intellectually challenging account of what actually happens in conflict and a no-nonsense guide to the practice of mediation, look no further. Victoria Pynchon is amazingly brilliant, deeply creative, profoundly insightful, and painfully honest. Read it. You won't be sorry."

Kenneth Cloke

Author of "The Crossroads of Conflict: A Journey into the Heart of Dispute Resolution", and "Conflict Revolution: Mediating Evil, War, Injustice and Terrorism"

———————

"The FCC might take issue with a chunk of these alphabetic words of prose, but the wisdom behind them landed me a chunk of change at the negotiating table."

Judy Martin

Founder WorkLifeNation.com, National Public Radio Contributor

———————

"A is for Ambitious, B is for Brilliant, C is for Creative, D is for Daring and E is for Enlightening. Vickie Pynchon has taken the very complex styles of negotiation that mediators see and wrestle with every day and boiled them down to a fun, simple read that is as educational and strategic as it is entertaining. This book should be on every business person's desk as a reference. And what a great client gift! Just avoid the temptation to bookmark the page that describes the recipient!

Do NOT open this book if you are faint of heart! Vickie pulls no punches. Even the illustrations are scary! We all know the people in this book. I could almost take a pen and write a name next to each one (including several names on the 'A' page). Vickie tells it like it is - the good, the bad and the ugly of negotiation, manipulation and persuasion styles employed by rookies and seasoned veterans alike. Want to understand how to negotiate for more? Read this book tonight!

Vickie Pynchon is one of the funniest and most brilliant people I know. As a lawyer-turned-mediator, she has gone back to school - both to get her L.LM in conflict resolution, and her PhD in the school of hard knocks. Combining her keen academic perspective with her gut busting experiences with lawyers and business people at her mediation table, Vickie distills negotiation styles down into easily digestible and memorable personalities that will stay with you long after you have devoured the book."

Lee Jay Berman

Mediator and founder of the American Institute of Mediation

———————

"The humorous title should not mislead the reader. This book is full of deep insights and truths about destructive and constructive conflict. Its informal and easy to read style make its profound wisdom available to the casual reader, not willing to plow through stuffy academic literature. This book offers field tested strategies for all of us as we negotiate the conflicts that make life rich, and sometimes painful."

Peter Robinson

Co-Director, Straus Institute of Dispute Resolution,
Pepperdine University School of Law

———————

"When I first met Victoria Pynchon, she was running with the big dogs – an A-list attorney, she was a top litigator in a litigious society. She had smashed the glass ceiling, made partner, and was flying first class. So when she quit to become a mediator, I admit I was dismayed. With her knack for winning, why would she want to help people just . . . settle? Because Vickie, a true visionary, understands what we've been missing. Why does someone have to lose in order for someone else to win? What if everybody wins? As a top mediator, teacher, mentor, and now the author of this essential book, Vickie Pynchon provides us with those tools. No matter who you are or where you're going, you gotta get this book!"

Rita Williams

Author of "If the Creek Don't Rise"

———————

"The ABCs of Conflict Resolution" is a great book on dispute resolution. Ms. Pynchon uses real world examples to provide excellent insight into the psychology and deeper understanding of disputes in a way that can be used and understood by anyone, whether a lawyer, professional mediator, employer or spouse. I highly recommend the book."

Christopher G. Hill, Esq.

Member, Virginia's Legal Elite in Construction Law and
author Construction Law Musings Blog

———————

"Combining personal anecdotes with real life situations we can all relate to, Ms. Pynchon has managed to elucidate the basic factors necessary to recognize a conflict and what skills enable us to deal with one when it arises. This book is both entertaining and thought provoking in that it encourages the reader to evaluate his/her own role in the creation, interpretation and resolution of conflict."

Angela S. Haskins, Esq.

Litigation partner at Baker, Keener & Nahra, LLP and former Director of the AAA Center for Mediation and Principal of ADR International, Inc.

———————

"Conflict is inevitable, but combat is optional". So says the old adage. Reality and practice of course are different: for anyone who has ever been locked tight inside it, conflict seems inescapable, with combat its inevitable expression. Dispute resolution practitioner, author, scholar, and negotiation expert Victoria Pynchon understands this. In her newest book, The ABCs of Conflict Resolution, Pynchon, a former trial warrior, draws upon her experiences as both lawyer and healer of conflict to offer readers a way to reclaim humanity and restore dignity to life's most vexing moments. With unflinching self-honesty, compassion for human frailty, and a healthy dose of humor, Pynchon masterfully brings us to reconciliation with ourselves and others."

Diane Levin, Esq.

Author of the Mediation Channel (www.mediationchannel.com) and the World Directory of ADR Blogs.

———————

The Grownups' ABCs of Conflict Resolution | 2nd Edition

Copyright ©2010 by Victoria Pynchon

Pynchon, Victoria, 1952-
The Grownups' ABCs of Conflict Resolution | 2nd Edition
With illustrations by Dean Murray

ISBN 978-0615831725

First Edition printing: October 2010

Second Edition printing: June 2013

Publisher: She Negotiates Press
　　　　www.shenegotiates.com

Editor: Rod Chapman, www.rodchapman.com
Book design: Kenneth Chew
Illustrations: Dean Murray, www.deanmurray.com
Photography: Sammy Davis, www.sammydavisphotography.com

The Grownups' ABCs of Conflict Resolution | 2nd Edition

with illustrations by Dean Murray

Victoria Pynchon, J.D., LL.M.

For my husband Stephen Goldberg, my Zen Master

TABLE OF CONTENTS

About Victoria Pynchon

Victoria Pynchon is the co-founder of She Negotiates Consulting and Training, a negotiation training and consulting service for women professionals, executives, managers, and entrepreneurs. Victoria received her LL.M. degree in Dispute Resolution from the Straus Institute, Pepperdine University School of Law in 2006, and her JD degree, Order of the Coif, in 1980 from The Martin Luther King, Jr. School of Law at the University of California, Davis. Though no longer practicing law, she cannot yet let go of her license to practice "before all the Courts of the State of California," as well as the federal district courts located in that state and the Ninth Circuit Court of Appeal. Ms. Pynchon currently lives in Los Angeles with her husband, Stephen Goldberg.

You can connect with Victoria Pynchon at:

www.shenegotiates.com

Acknowledgements

As Joseph Campbell wrote, when you reach a certain age and look back over your lifetime,

> *it can seem to have had a consistent order and plan, as though composed by some novelist. Events that when they occurred had seemed accidental and of little moment turn out to have been indispensable factors in the composition of a consistent plot. So who composed that plot? Schopenhauer suggests that just as your dreams are composed by an aspect of yourself of which your consciousness is unaware, so, too, your whole life is composed by the will within you. And just as people whom you will have met apparently by mere chance became leading agents in the structuring of your life, so, too, will you have served unknowingly as an agent, giving meaning to the lives of others. The whole thing gears together like one big symphony, with everything unconsciously structuring everything else. And Schopenhauer concludes that it is as though our lives were the features of the one great dream of a single dreamer in which all the dream characters dream, too; so that everything links to everything else, moved by the one will to life which is the universal will in nature.*

I begin with the leading agent of this book. He is the grace note that begins the symphony of the book and is its final melody. He has been the book's biggest noodge ("how's the book coming?") and its most enthusiastic cheerleader. He is my husband Stephen N. Goldberg. Stephen and I stumbled upon one another in my second decade of legal practice, each of us representing different axes of evil (petroleum and insurance) in an environmental insurance coverage dispute. Years later, love arrived, beginning my personal quest for dispute resolution that did not include cross-examination at the breakfast table.

It was Stephen who gave me both the courage to write my first book and its title. I walked into the kitchen one sunny Southern California morning to find him, as usual, reading the early edition of the *Los Angeles Times* before heading off to work. I'd been blogging for a while and the thought of writing a book follows a blog like night follows day.

"I think I could write an ABC's of Conflict Resolution," I said without bothering with any morning pleasantries. Without a pause, Stephen responded with "A is for Asshole." The rest is this minor history.

Friends pre-exist, endure, and follow marriage. Truly, nothing whatsoever could be accomplished without them. Dr. Anne LaBorde is this book's best friend and and my soul sister. When the conversation veers into the sort of girl talk that involves how frustrating men can be, it is Anne who reminds me that Stephen is my Zen Master. To Anne, I dedicate the letter Z.

Stephen's loving support aside, I still would never have had the courage to write a book of any kind without the love and support of my writers' group, a more loyal and constant group of friends than I ever imagined having. If the book is free of awkward phrases, lapses into irrelevant detail, and stultifying prose, much of the credit goes to these generous people who patiently listened to and commented on many early drafts. In the twenty years I've been part of this glorious group of writers, we have all published. Some in the small literary press and collections of short fiction (Birute Serota); some in hauntingly beautiful and deeply felt memoirs (Rita Williams and Jackie Gorman); one in an award winning novella that could make Faulkner weep (Emmy-award winning lyricist, Kathleen Wakefield); and teacher, actor and writer Russel Lundy whose WWII novel has not been published only because he cannot seem to let it go. Jan Bramlett, who introduced me to this extraordinary group of people has since left town to perform her lyric work with her voice and her guitar. To all of these generous and talented people, I dedicate the letter "C" which stands not only for Coward, but also for Courage.

Just about everything I know about the constructive resolution of conflict I learned at the Straus Institute for Dispute Resolution at the Pepperdine University School of Law in Malibu, California. The teachers and mentors who schooled me there and whose wisdom appears throughout much of this book include Peter Robinson and Tom Stipanowich, Co-Directors of the Institute; Richard C. Reuben, Professor of Law and the social psychology of conflict at the University of Missouri-Columbia School of Law; Dan Van Ness, Director of the Prison Fellowship International's Centre for Justice and Reconciliation (directly responsible for the chapter V is for Victim);

Maureen Weston, Pepperdine's negotiation queen; Larry Sullivan, inter-religious dispute resolution guru; former labor negotiator and externship guide James Stott; transformative mediation guru Joe Folger; Jack McCrory, brilliant and gentle guide to all LL.M students; and the Rev. Brian Cox who taught me that intractable ethnic, racial and religious disputes could be resolved by having "conversations of the heart" that touch on the historic wounds that make these conflicts persist and too often to explode into violence. To these wise and generous teachers, I dedicate the chapter M is for Mediator.

I began to blog on ADR topics in 2006 when I stumbled over local mediator Jeff Krivis' blog (thanks Jeff!) I've often said that the blogosphere is a small Midwestern town where the residents feel safe enough to keep their doors unlocked at night and everyone has carte blanche to walk into the neighbors' kitchens, open their refrigerators and taste whatever gustatory pleasures await their curiosity. Chief among my guides and colleagues in this generous and collaborative world was and is the brilliant and savvy Diane Levin whose Mediation Channel and World Directory of ADR Blogs set the standard high enough to keep me blogging in an effort to reach it. Others in the blogosphere who directly or indirectly contributed to the book include Tammy Lenski (Conflict Zen), Stephanie West Allen (Idealawg and Brains on Purpose), Geoff Sharp (formerly of Mediator Blah Blah and now of the m3 blog); John DeGroote (Settlement Perspectives); Jan Frankel Schau (Schau's Mediation), Phyllis Pollack (PGP Mediation Blog), Jeff Thompson (Enjoy Mediation), Karl Bayer, Victoria VanBuren, and Holly Hayes (Disputing Blog), Lee Jay Berman (Eye On Conflict Blog) and the Professors behind the ADR Prof Blog (Andrea Schneider, Michael Moffitt, Sarah Cole, Art Hinshaw, Jill Gross, and Cynthia Alkon). No list of mediation writers would be complete without Jim Melamed, founder of mediate.com, which published my first mediation article back in 2005. They provide a home for mediators and the work that mediators do with passion, pride and the promise of a better tomorrow. To these wonderful folks I dedicate the chapter N is for Neighbor.

Special thanks also goes to anonymous Ed. of Blawg Review for whom I spent many happy months as a "sherpa," finding and recommending the best law blog posts of the week for inclusion of that mainstay of the legal blogosphere. Though I personally know Ed. to be bold and forthright, because he has remained anonymous all of these years, I am irresistibly drawn to dedicate to him the chapter P is for Paranoid.

My fellow Straus classmates also contributed to this book and to my own sanity in a time of career upheaval. Chief among them is lawyer, mediator, and peacemaker John Shafer who "went down the rabbit hole" of ADR in 2004 and continues to ask which way is "up." It is to John that I dedicate the chapter F for Friend. Other classmates who were necessary reactors in the nuclear core of the Straus Institute's conflict resolution power plant include Scott Badenoch, Rebecca Callahan, Robert Wrede, Andrew Cochrane, Dorit Cypis, Kathleen Dillon and others too numerous to name. What these students share is a lively curiosity about the human condition. To them I dedicate the chapter Q is for Questioner.

Three Judges of the Los Angeles Superior Court have a special place in this book as they do in my mediation training. They are the Judges with whom I apprenticed while earning my LL.M degree and who taught me the vast range of mediation practices from evaluative to directive, transformative to persuasive, and ingratiating to coercive. They are Associate Justice Victoria Chaney of the California Court of Appeal, Second Appellate District; the Hon. Carl West of the Los Angeles Superior Complex Court; and, the Hon. Alexander Williams, III (ret.) who formerly presided in the Los Angeles Superior Court's Settlement Department. To them I dedicate the chapter J is for Judge.

There is a community of women ADR neutrals in Los Angeles without whom it would be impossible to maintain my peace of mind and improve my skills at the same time. Chief among them is attorney, mediator, and arbitrator, Deborah Rothman, who took me under her wing when she was serving as Chair of the ADR Section of the Beverly Hills Bar Association. Deborah taught me everything she knew about the theory and practice of arbitration and mediation, shared with me her extensive network of women neutrals, and bucked me up whenever I worried that mediation had not been the right choice to make. Two other (among dozens) of women mediators who welcomed me to the practice with open arms were Jan Frankel Schau and Laurel Kaufer. The rest of the Fabulous Women Neutrals know who they are and how grateful I am for their encouragement and good will.

Other women central to the writing of the book have come into my life far more recently. They are the students and clients of She Negotiates Consulting and Training, a venture that has taken off like Fourth of July fireworks thanks to the happy partnership between me and certified Life Coach, artist, journalist, actor, mother and friend, Lisa Gates. Every woman who we have trained, to whom we have spoken, and with whom we have consulted has deepened my appreciation of what women can accomplish once they learn their market value, and then proceed to name it and claim it. Of special note are those women in our first Negotiation Master class: Whitney Johnson, Cali Yost, Chrysula Winegar, Judy Martin, and Trudie Olsen Curtis. This list would not be complete without the women who wrote the *She Negotiates* column for Forbes Woman magazine: Lisa Gates, Katie Phillips, Roxana Popescu, Brooke Axtel, and Chelsea Aiken. Everlasting gratitude to the women who made that column possible: Sharon Gitelle, Francesca Donner, and Caroline Howard.

To all of these women ~ both the ADR neutrals and the members of the She Negotiates community ~ I dedicate the chapter W is for Women.

Others who have been "leading agents in the structuring of [my] life" and hence of this book include my former husband Joel M. Deutsch who first encouraged me to write as if my life depended upon it (as indeed it has); attorney, poet and musician Joseph Mockus (who taught me how to read literature when we were fellow Lit Majors at U.C. San Diego); Carol Fuerth, who more or less forced me to attend a women's consciousness raising class at San Diego's Center for Women's Studies and Services in 1974; sobriety guide and mentor, the poet and teacher Kris McHaddad, attorney, author, professor, mediator, and activist Dr. Kenneth Cloke; mediator, teacher and American Mediation Institute founder, Lee Jay Berman, and, the recently passed and greatly missed attorney, mediator, former cavalry officer and Yoda of the Los Angeles mediation scene, Richard Millen.

Lisa Gates (who of necessity appears in these acknowledgements more than once) read the entire manuscript, applied to it her considerable literary editorial wisdom and helped me finally let it go on its third or fourth complete revision. Editor Rob Chapman, resident in Paris, France, also provided expert editorial guidance on more than one draft. Ray Sobol of Reason Press, who so generously shepherded me through the (exhausting and frustrating) process of turning half-formed ideas and incoherent ramblings into an actual book is the source of everything good here. I formally absolve him of anything less than worthy. To them, and unnamed others who gambled on this book, including illustrator Dean Murray, I dedicate the chapter G is for Gambler.

Special thanks go to those writers and artists who permitted their work to be used to illustrate the courageous efforts now being undertaken to replace a punitive adversarial system with processes that recognize our human fallibility and the possibility of redemption for everyone. V is for Victim is drawn almost entirely from the brilliant and inspiring documentary *Beyond Conviction* directed and produced by Rachel Libert, co-founder of Tied to the Tracks Films, a production company dedicated to the creation of films that raise awareness and effect social change. Thank you Ms. Libert for providing me with a transcript of that film and granting us permission to draw inspiration and story from it here. Attorney, mediator, activist, author and founder of Mediators Beyond Borders, Dr. Kenneth Cloke, also permitted us to quote the sage advice he has left for us in several books as a bread crumb trail to find our way to peace with justice.

Because this book exists only because I have been given the privilege of entering the lives of people in active dispute ~ people with the courage to sit down with their presumed enemies to engage and resolve rather than to avoid often painful conflict ~ I thank the institutions that made and make these difficult conversations possible

~ the Los Angeles Superior Court's ADR Program; the United States District Court's (Central District of California) Settlement Officer Program; the Los Angeles County Bar Association's Dispute Resolution Program; the West Hollywood DRS Community Mediation Center (particularly its former director, Kathryn Turk) Judicate West ADR Services and its ADR professionals Alan Brutman, Var Fox and Rosemarie Chiusano, and the indefatigable Lucie Baron of ADR Services, Inc.

Finally, I must thank my mother Lois Borden, who taught me all of the core values of peacemaking: tolerance; understanding; constructive conversations; patience; humor; and, most of all, an unconditional love for even the most troublesome among us.

Los Angeles, 2013

Introduction

Welcome to the *ABCs of Conflict Resolution,* a primer on the resolution of disputes ranging from the neighbor's barking dog to the man with a bomb in his shoe. Whether we're trying to understand the most recent outbreak of violence in the Middle East or to negotiate our way out of a cell-phone contract, the principles and practices used by international diplomats, school principals, Wall Street executives, corporate lawyers, and used car salesmen, are the same. It's time for these negotiation and dispute-resolution skills to come out of the universities, get up from the seats of power, walk out of the halls of justice and into your community, your neighborhood, and your home. It's time for all of us to pick up the peacemaker's toolkit and begin building the kind of world in which we would all prefer to live.

The first chapter, A is for Asshole, is a hologram of the entire book. It tells a familiar story of conflict and explains that assholes are not people but behaviors, and not one person but two. Like all conflicts that erupt into name-calling, the use of the word asshole signals the existence of a relationship in crisis. Why that crisis occurs and how it can best be managed is summarized at the end of the chapter.

The chapters D is for Drama Queen, F is for Friend and N is for Neighbor explore disruptions in relationships among workers, pals and neighbors. The chapters J is for Judge, L is for Lawyer and M is for Mediator recount stories in which third parties attempt to resolve the conflicts presented to them for resolution. Other chapters explain why some people become heroes (H is for Heroes), why families help their own (K is for Kin), and why the efforts of so many good-hearted people to bring peace onto the field fail so spectacularly, as Romeo learned in Shakespeare's exploration of teenage love across enemy lines.

Other chapters deal with the difficult people who populate our lives – the bullies, enemies and idiots who defy our understanding and madden us to violence or tears (B, E and I). Several of the chapters explain why and how we reflexively address conflict – by avoiding or suppressing it (C is for Coward), courting it (G is for Gambler), rectifying it (O is for Outlaw), or transforming the relationships that arise out of it (V is for Victim). Some letters of the conflict resolution alphabet explain the cognitive biases that too often prevent us from making sound decisions, such as

"P is for Paranoid" and "X is for Xenophobe," while others (T is for Them and U is for Us) describe the many ways in which we try, but too often fail, to make peace with our fellows.

The story of my own transformation from fire-breathing trial warrior to collaborative problem solver and negotiation consultant is the subject of the chapter "M is for Mediator." Today, with a thirty-year legal career behind me, I am an author, keynote speaker, and negotiation trainer and consultant with the firm I co-founded: She Negotiates Consulting and Training. The stories of disputes among businesses, lawyers, executives and entrepreneurs arise from my work life. Other, more mundane but no less important conflict stories, are the ones told to me as a volunteer in my local community mediation center. This is my most gratifying work, helping those who are bold enough and brave enough sit down with warring neighbors, spouses, family members, landlords and employers in an effort to achieve peace.

People just like them arrive in church basements and community recreation centers all over the country to meet with neighbors whose dogs bark until three a.m., whose landlords fail to fix their leaking faucets, and whose former spouses refuse to stop smoking marijuana in front of the kids. The stories of these mediations, as well as those at which I now make my living, also populate the pages of this book.

Just as a child's primer first introduces us to the alphabet upon which all of our future learning will be based, the *ABCs of Conflict Resolution* is meant to provide a strong foundation upon which to build a future of competent conflict resolution skills. Each letter provides advice for resolving common disputes that arise in our daily lives. Most remind us that the crisis of conflict is also an opportunity to address inequities, clarify our values and promote the general well being of our families, communities, states and nations. For that reason, the book not only gives instruction in negotiation, litigation and mediation, it also provides tools that readers can immediately put to use as they walk themselves and their fellows through the conflicts that baffle and the disputes that plague us all.

If the conflict alphabet had a single message, it would be this – despite our diversity of interests, apparent scarcity of resources and seemingly conflicting values, we can and must pick up the tools of accountability, forgiveness and reconciliation to survive. Having read and taken the lessons of this book to heart, I hope that you will be able to use them to speak to your estranged children, to calmly discuss a family member's decision to change religions, to persuasively press your case for a raise in pay, to bring peace into a room of quarrelsome co-workers, and to protect yourself and your family against the demands of bullies.

I leave you to it, in the expectation that with a bit of practice you will soon be able to use the insights gained here on those too-frequent occasions when conflict erupts into acrimony. May you learn to be comfortable with ambiguity, flexible and intuitive in dialogue, and attentive to the commonalities that unite you with your fellows. May you be alert to the cry for help that seeks expression behind every accusation. Most of all, I hope you will practice seeking out some small part of yourself, no matter how insignificant, in every person you meet.

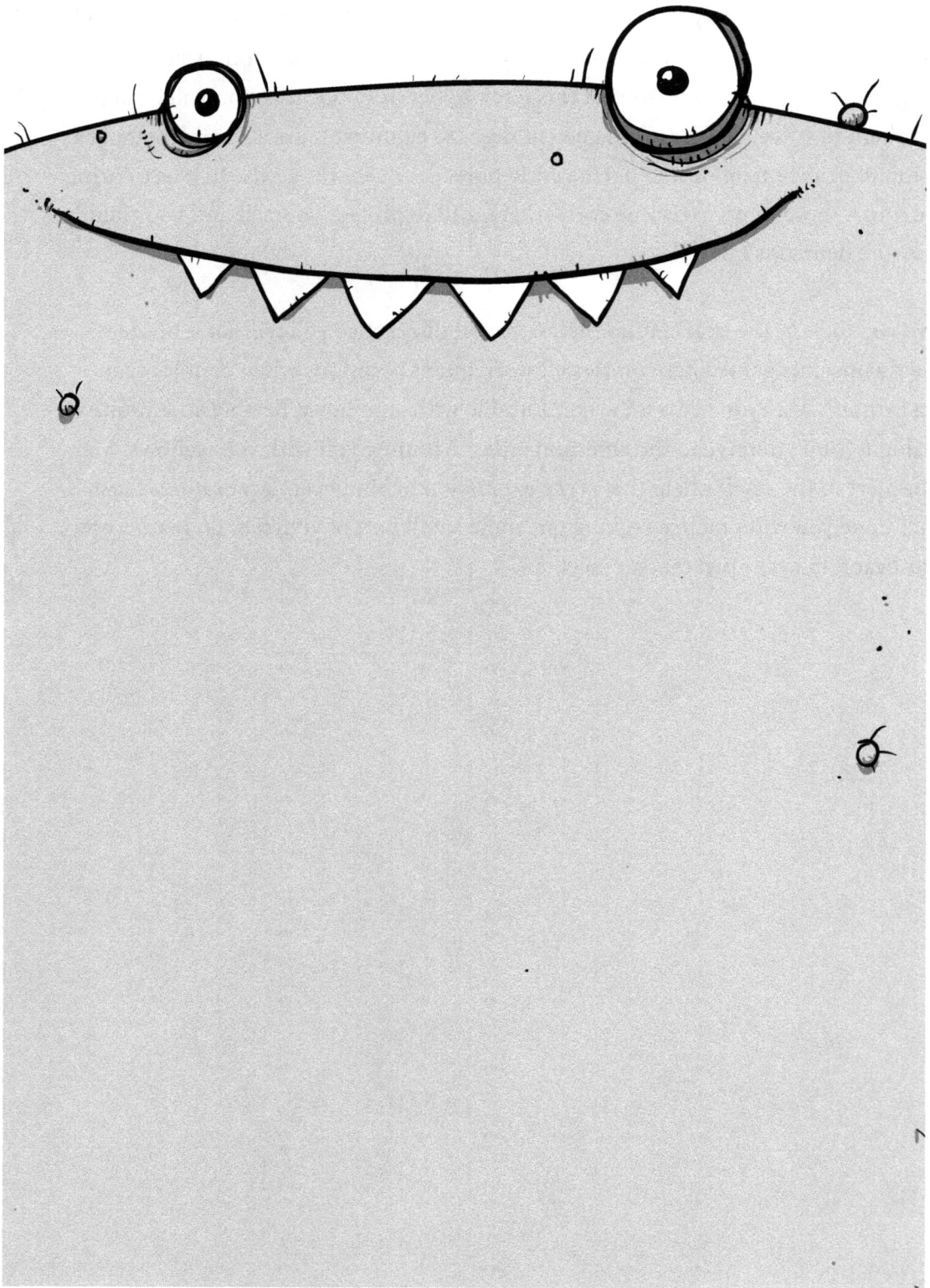

A

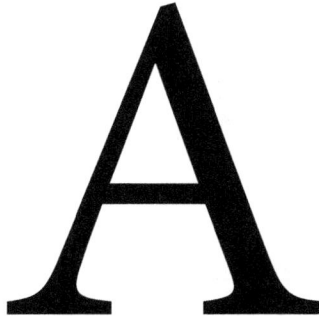

A is for Asshole

You recognize this guy.

He's the one who stole your parking place. He cut you off in traffic. Just last night at the Olmstead's party, he interrupted your story about your trip to London for the sole purpose of changing the subject to his trip to Cambodia.

You, on the other hand, are not an asshole. You are respectful of other people's property, return telephone calls promptly, and honor the compacts that grease the wheels of social interaction. These compacts are mostly rules of etiquette, some of which have been turned into law—such as "first in time, first in right."

Still, you're not inflexible. You can make the reasonable exception. If you're standing in the checkout line with a shopping cart carrying enough food to feed a family of ten for a month, you don't say no to the young woman holding a bottle of spring water when she asks if she can cut in front of you. If you refuse her this reasonable courtesy, you are the asshole.

Thus we learn that an asshole is not necessarily a person or even a behavior. No one can be an asshole alone in his room. He needs someone to be an asshole to. An asshole is a social relationship in crisis. An asshole is a dispute.

Let's go back to the asshole who steals your parking space.

It's Christmastime at the Farmers' Market in Los Angeles. Although the day is warm and the mood festive, the afternoon sun is reflecting harshly against your windshield as you make your third circuit of the parking lot. You're getting tense. You need to pick up the kids after soccer practice. If you don't find a place right now you'll have to turn around and leave, your errand undone.

You're not alone in this contemporary hunting-and-gathering adventure. If you were, you would already have slid your Honda SUV into one of the many available spaces, picked up the ornaments you need to finish trimming the tree, and be headed over to the soccer field right now—but it's not just you. At least ten other drivers are circling the lot and another five or six are patiently idling their cars in the aisles.

You think you're in a parking lot, but you're really in a field of conflict.

Conflict exists whenever one person believes that his needs or desires cannot be satisfied at the same time as those of his fellows. The social scientists who study these things call this "perceived relative deprivation." Each person searching for a parking space is deprived in relation to everyone whose cars fill the lot. Although someone might make a space available at any moment, it looks as if there are not enough parking places to accommodate your needs. Your deprivation is therefore both perceived (apparent, but not necessarily true) and relative (to those who have already parked their cars).

As frustrated as you might be, you are not angry with the people who found parking spaces before you, nor are you irritable with your fellow seekers. This is just how life is. You may be in competition for scarce resources, but nothing wrong or unfair has happened to you, at least not as far as you can tell. There is no one to name as the source of your deprivation, no one to blame for your current distress, and no one from whom to claim the right to a parking space. Until you are able to name, blame, and claim, there may be conflict, but there is no dispute.

Then, just as you've resigned yourself to leaving the lot with your errands undone, a young woman trailing two toddlers appears at the door of a blue Volvo just a few spaces ahead of you. She smiles and gives you a friendly wave to indicate she is leaving. Though inconsiderate shoppers have carelessly parked their cars over the lines, making the offered space an awfully tight fit, you're hoping you can successfully navigate your way into it. Your spirits pick up. The ornaments will be purchased and your children picked up on time. You're feeling all Christmas-y again. Relaxing behind the wheel of your car, you shift into neutral and switch on the radio.

However, just as the Volvo pulls out, a young man in a red Miata convertible swings around the corner and noses into *your* space. Maybe he didn't see you waiting for it. You suppress a flash of anger and shout, "Hey! That's my spot!"

You're really hoping he'll smile back, shrug his shoulders to indicate his mistake and yield it to you, the rightful possessor—but that's not what happens.

With one hand on his cell phone and the other on the steering wheel, Red lifts his left arm in a sweeping gesture that you interpret as waving away your concern. What you don't know is this: before Red slipped his car into your space, he saw another car begin to pull out three or four spaces ahead of you. Noticing that it was much larger than the one you were waiting for, Red quickly seized upon yours, gesturing you toward the better spot. You, however, are not looking ahead. Your eyes are burning into Red's back.

As he turns off his engine and jumps out of his car, you roll down your window and shout, "Asshole!" And with that angry epithet, an asshole is born.

Before now, there was no asshole. There may have been an awkward moment between two well-meaning, fair-minded people. You and Red might have shared rueful laughter, indicating empathy for one another's mutual plight. As Red backed his car out of your space, you might have apologized for shouting at him, blamed your irritation on the holidays, and wished him luck in finding his own space. He might have quickly forgiven your brief flash of ill temper and wished you a nice day. You would have been reconciled to life's little inconveniences, and to one another.

But that's not how it happened. Instead of resolving into apology, forgiveness, and reconciliation, that asshole stole your parking space! Red's refusal to cede your spot to you is the spark that transforms a conflict over scarce resources into an active dispute. Social scientists call this spark the "injurious event" that permits us to name someone else as the source of our deprivation, blame that person for taking from us that which is rightfully ours, and claim recompense for our loss.

Naming, blaming, and claiming. These are the necessary elements of all disputes, from a fight over a parking space to a war over national boundaries.

> *"Naming, blaming, and claiming. These are the necessary elements of all disputes, from a fight over a parking space to a war over national boundaries."*

Not until the word asshole fades into the chatter of Christmas shoppers drifting back from the mall do you see the newly available SUV-sized space. Red looks at you over his shoulder before bowing at the waist and sweeping his arm toward the open slot. Then he raises his index finger and wiggles it at you in the universal signal for misbehavior. You flush with embarrassment, chagrined at the strength of your anger and your lapse into profanity. Now you feel like the asshole. Why?

Because the resources you were competing for, though scarce, were in fact sufficient to simultaneously satisfy both your own and Red's needs. There was no genuine contest in the first place. The dispute was unnecessary—the result of misunderstanding rather than disrespect. You will live with its painful emotional residue for the remainder of the day. You were in a state of perceived—but not actual—deprivation. The conflict existed only in your head.

So what happened here? Let's review.

As soon as you entered the parking lot you were in a state of perceived relative deprivation, competing for scarce resources with at least fifteen other motorists. You were in the field of conflict. That conflict did not become a dispute until you suffered an injurious event—Red's "theft" of your parking space. At that moment, it appeared as if you and Red could not simultaneously meet your needs. Worse, it appeared that Red had wrongfully deprived you of the only parking resource left in the lot, thus breaking the social compact of first in time, first in right.

At the moment Red refused your demand for possession, you named him as the source of your injury, blamed him for your loss, and claimed a right to redress, all in a single profane epithet – asshole. Thus, both an asshole and a dispute emerged. Red was not behaving badly, he was actually engaged in an act of kindness that you understandably misinterpreted as being rude, boorish, and anti-social. The confrontation and the bad feeling that went with it were understandable, but unnecessary.

In the *Dispute Resolution ABCs*, A is for Asshole because an asshole is not a person but a process; not a character trait but a social interaction; not one person but two. A is for Asshole because the asshole is the dispute.

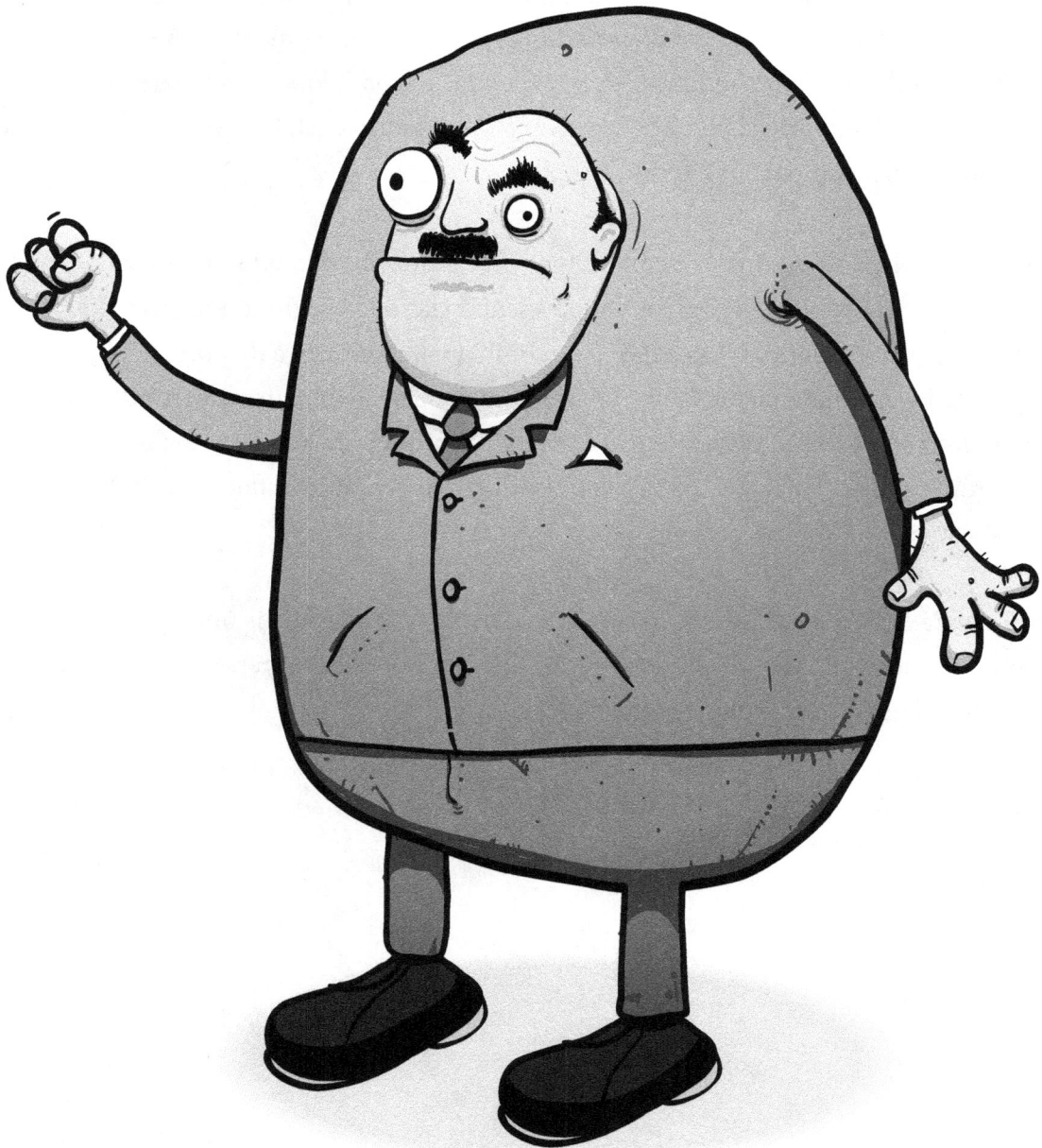

B

B is for Bully

Here's another familiar character. This is the kid who shook you down for your lunch money on the elementary school playground, the boy who taunted you in gym whenever you failed to pass the basketball to the only teammate able to sink it, and the swaggering delinquent who blew smoke in your face whenever you passed by.

Bullying is not, however, only the domain of the male animal. There's no bully quite as deadly as the high school girl who uses her newfound talent for empathy as a laser gun directed at her friends' fragile teenage hearts. While boys tend to use physical superiority to intimidate, girls use the "gentler" arts of ridicule, gossip, and shunning.

Like the asshole, no one can be a bully alone in her room. She needs someone to be a bully to. A bully is another relationship in crisis. Bullies inexplicably name victims as sources of discontent, blame those people for their unhappiness, and claim a right to retaliate.

Before we throw stones at our fellows, let's talk about the only bully whose behavior we can control—*us*. We're leaders in our communities: presidents of the elementary school PTA, den mothers to Brownie and Cub Scout troops, leaders of homeowners' associations, and frequent donors to charitable causes. We keep our houses in good repair, our lawns watered and mowed, and our children neatly dressed.

Still, we are human and fallible. Just yesterday one of us—Crystal—had a run-in with her neighbor, Jane. Crystal and Jane have daughters in a Brownie Troupe for which Crystal serves as Den Mother. Crystal is also the President of the PTA. Crystal has been asking Jane to trim back the limbs of her lemon tree ever since they began to grow over Crystal's fence more than a year ago. Now, the tree is dropping its overripe lemons into Crystal's fish pond and it's making her irritable.

"I'm afraid one of those lemons will kill my fish," Crystal says with good humor one morning as she and Jane run into one another on the sidewalk. "Don't you think it's time to finally trim that tree?"

Jane looks harried and responds defensively, listing for Crystal the obligations she must satisfy that same day, and concluding, between clenched teeth, "I don't have a man around the house to help, like you do."

You should be able to see the dispute coming now. Jane is in a state of perceived relative deprivation. Crystal has something she doesn't have—a husband to help around the house—but there's no fault attached to anyone within the field of conflict yet. Yet.

Few of us actually enjoy the escalation of a conflict into an active dispute. Jane and Crystal are no exception. There's no telling how further face-to-face discussions about the tree and its errant fruit might end. The rules of polite conversation could be suddenly suspended. Jane might shout at Crystal or insult her. Things could wheel completely out of control. Hoping to avoid an emotional confrontation, Crystal turns to email, telling Jane that the overhanging branches of the lemon tree are a "nuisance" that Crystal is hoping Jane will "abate."

Crystal's use of formal legal language makes her feel knowledgeable and powerful. She's hoping it will make Jane comply. Unfortunately, that's not what happens. Jane is beginning to feel bullied and like the rest of us, she doesn't like doing anything at the point of a gun. Two weeks later, Crystal ups the ante by sending Jane a registered letter threatening to take Jane to small claims court if she refuses to comply with Crystal's demand within thirty days. Now Jane is burning with anger and resentment. The women avoid one another on the street and at school functions. They're both angry, bitter, and miserable.

One morning at three a.m., Crystal crawls out of bed to surf the Internet for advice. Her efforts take her to BadNeighbors.com—an online community bulletin board containing hundreds of complaints about barking dogs, dilapidated yards, and kids playing basketball after nine p.m. Some people have followed up their original posts with expressions of gratitude, saying that their complaints were resolved quickly after they'd been posted online.

"Perfect," thinks Crystal as she begins tapping out a description of her dilemma with Jane—the tree and its overhanging branches, the effect it has had on her peace of mind, her attempts to get Jane to live up to her responsibilities, and Jane's responses— right down to the comment about not having a husband. Crystal not only includes Jane's full name in her post, she also mentions the street on which they both live. Crystal's finger hovers over the send button even as her conscience urges her not to hit it. Crystal feels powerless and put upon. Lodging this public complaint only seems fair. She hits send and forwards the link to Jane and Crystal's mutual friends.

Crystal awakens the following morning feeling regret. It briefly occurs to her that she's bullying Jane. But isn't Crystal the one who is right here? Why should she feel guilty? In an effort to force Jane to do something she's said she cannot do, Crystal has used every contentious (i.e., manipulative) dispute resolution tactic in the book, except violence. First, she ingratiated herself with Crystal, admitting her anxiety about the lemons falling into Crystal's fish pond. Her bid for sympathy was, however, harshly rebuffed, resulting first in a request for assistance, then in a legal threat, and finally in an act of public shaming.

The use of these contentious dispute resolution tactics do not, however, qualify as bullying. Bullying occurs when one person deliberately and repeatedly abuses a position of power over another to compel compliance with a demand, and generally occurs in social settings with a clear hierarchy and little or no supervision. Clear hierarchies create positions of power that can be abused and the absence of supervision permits a superior player to dominate the inferior without negative social consequences. Though Crystal and Jane are neither coworkers nor grade-schoolers, Crystal's positions of authority (Brownies, PTA) enable her to shame Jane in an attempt to compel compliance with her demands, and Crystal has used the unsupervised power of the Internet to do so—a relatively new form of coercion called "cyber-bullying."

The most curious shared attributes of both the bully and the bullied is their mutual feelings of powerlessness and oppression. That's how Crystal felt when Jane rebuffed her request to trim her tree. Now Jane is being harassed by what feels like the entire community.

A bully, like an asshole, is a social relationship in crisis. It arises from an injurious event in which one person names another as the source of a problem (encroaching tree limbs over the fence, lemons in the fish pond), finds a basis for blame (Jane's refusal to cut back tree limbs that create a nuisance on Crystal's property), and makes a claim for redress (trim the darn tree). Fair enough, you say, but what's the solution?

If you think back on Crystal's initial conversation with Jane about the tree, you'll hear Jane describing the circumstances that motivate her inaction. On the morning Crystal and Jane first spoke about the lemons, Jane said she was feeling overwhelmed with work and more than a little envious of Crystal's married state. Instead of asking Jane if she needed help trimming back the tree, Crystal began a course of conduct meant to force Jane to do what she might not have had the power to do.

One of the ways a mediator helps people resolve disputes is to first ask about their motivations (sometimes called "interests") and then to help them brain storm solutions that don't require either party to be "right" and with which both parties can comply without a great burden to either one or the other. If Jane can neither trim the tree herself nor afford to pay a tree-trimmer, someone else in the neighborhood—perhaps Crystal's husband—might be willing to volunteer a couple of hours of his time to do so. In the spirit of neighborly gratitude and cooperation, Jane might cook up a mid-morning brunch for the generous men or women who offer to bring a ladder and a chain saw to cut back the intruding limbs of the lemon tree. Under the best of circumstances, both women would apologize to the other for her part in the dispute, forgive one another their common human fallibility, and reconcile. After all, permitting the dispute to go on unresolved will continue to make both women uncomfortable at school events and wary of running into one another when they return home at the end of the day. No lawsuit or group pressure will ease the burden an active dispute inevitably imposes on those forced to suffer it.

Let's review:

A bully, like an asshole, is not a person, but a behavior and not one person, but two. Because bullies operate in social settings with clear hierarchies and little or no supervision, it is difficult to resolve a bullying problem on your own. Third parties trained in dispute resolution can equalize the imbalance

> *"Because bullies operate in social settings with clear hierarchies and little or no supervision, it is difficult to resolve a bullying problem on your own."*

of power that allows one person to victimize another, and provide the supervision necessary to bring the troublesome conduct back into line with civilized norms.

In the *ABCs of Conflict Resolution*, bullies and victims regain control over their own lives by taking responsibility for the part they play in the bully-bullied dynamic, coming together to identify and resolve the real problem causing the bad behavior, apologizing to one another for misunderstandings and over-reactions, making amends for the harm done, forgiving one another, and reconciling. In the *ABCs of Conflict Resolution*, these steps toward reconciliation are never easy to initiate, but once begun, they rarely fail.

C

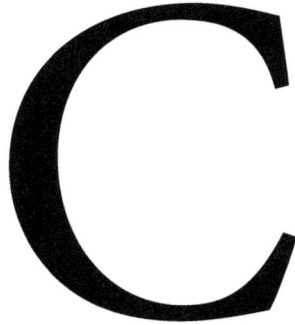

C is for Coward

You'd never call this guy a coward. He's a rock climber, river rafter, and a member of the National Guard. During the Gulf War he served his country as a paratrooper for goodness sakes. He's a hero. And yet, on this warm and sunny Southern California morning, the guy behind the coatrack is not acting the hero. He's behaving like a coward. Why?

See that willowy blonde paying for a vintage t-shirt at the counter? That's Mary. Charles the Coward was one of Mary's classmates ten years ago. Mary, like Charles, is a screenwriter. When she finished her first screenplay last year, she sent it to Charles, who was working as a writer on a popular sit-com. She's asked Charles for his opinion about her work.

Charles meant to get around to reading Mary's script—he always liked her—but so many people send Charles their plays, novels, poems, and scripts, and so many of them are unreadable, that the thought of another one was just too much to bear. Besides, when Mary's screenplay had arrived in his mailbox, he'd been working fourteen-hour days. He really didn't have the time.

 Now, crouched uncomfortably behind a rack of polyester jogging suits in the heat of a summer day, Charles is hiding and feeling foolish.

What's going on here?

Charles is avoiding conflict, as we're all prone to do. Sometime during toddlerhood we learn that our needs and our family's needs will not always be simultaneously met. This divergence of "interests" (needs, desires, preferences, and priorities) is what we've already learned conflict to be. We also learn early on that conflict can turn into a frightening dispute at the drop of a hat. We spill our milk on mom's new dress. She slaps our hand. We burst into tears and are sent into our room. Later, we push a fellow grade-schooler off the jungle gym and are deprived of recess privileges for a week. Sometimes the teacher shames us by sending us to the principal or making us stand outside in the hall. It's safer, we've learned, and easier, we've concluded, just to avoid conflict altogether. The social scientists say that we've all become "conflict averse."

What Charles doesn't know about the conflict playing out in his head is this: at the same time Mary sent the script to Charles, she also sent it to the friend of a friend of a famous Hollywood producer. The producer acquired Mary's script for a serious sum of money. At this very moment the movie is in pre-production while Mary works on a second screenplay in the three-picture deal she negotiated with Paramount. If Charles weren't hiding behind the clothes rack, he'd learn that Mary has been searching for someone to punch up her current script—a job that is perfect for Charles, who has been out of work for several months. Mary has completely forgotten that she ever sent Charles' a copy of her screenplay. She often thinks of him fondly and wonders how his career is doing. She also wonders why he never calls.

Charles' response to conflict is costing him not only a valuable friendship, but also an important professional opportunity. Even if Mary were to chide Charles for failing to get back to her, the potential rewards are so much greater than the likely pain of censure that it would do Charles—and all of us—good to use opportunities like this to practice the resolution of conflict.

Charles' crime, after all, is simply a breach of etiquette. It's polite to respond to a party invitation and impolite to leave the host wondering how many plates to put on the dinner table, or how

> *"Coward is a strong word, but so is the word courage."*

many party hats to buy for her child's birthday party. Though merely matters of polite behavior, breaches of these conventions have been known to sunder family relations, stop romance in its tracks, and stymie business partnerships.

Coward is a strong word, but so is the word courage. It takes courage to acknowledge wrongdoing—even so minor a misstep as failing to respond to a friend's request for assistance. Coming out from behind the clothing rack to explain a misdeed is, however, more liberation than obligation. Pity poor Charles, living in shame and remorse for a slight that Mary does not even recall. A heartfelt apology for a small act of disrespect can reestablish Charles' personal and professional relationship with Mary to the benefit of both. In the *ABCs of Conflict*, C stands not only for Coward, but also for the courage it takes to acknowledge our human fallibility, acknowledge wrongdoing, make amends, and reconcile with our fellows.

D

D is Drama Queen

Here's another character everyone will recognize the Drama Queen. Male or female, the Drama Queen stirs the pot of conflict to add emotional intensity and intrigue to an otherwise ordinary business day.

Of the primary responses to conflict—denying, avoiding, yielding, problem solving, and contending—Drama Queens almost always choose contention. As we noted in "B is for Bully," contentious responses to conflict include ingratiation or gamesmanship, shaming, threats, promises or arguments, and coercive commitments or violence. All of these tactics are employed to overpower the will of another and get what we want.

Drama Queen John is a colleague recently assigned to work on the same project as you. John is impulsive, chaotic, inefficient, and unproductive. You are calm, well-organized, efficient, and productive. You've never understood why John has lasted as long as he has at his job. As a good team player, you've been keeping your own counsel. You've mentioned neither your opinions about John nor your irritation with him to your coworkers. In all your dealings with him you've been careful not to show annoyance. You've been getting along and going along, while at the same time trying to keep your eye on the prize—the successful completion of the project entrusted to you.

But for all your caution, things started to go wrong on the first day the team met. That afternoon, your supervisor, Jamie, dropped by your office to mention that your teammate, Gina, complained about your domineering style. The following week, you overheard George saying you didn't deserve the bonus you received last year. Someone else suggested that you have a "special" relationship with the divisional vice president. By week three, your team meetings had become tense. People with whom you had worked well for a long time began eyeing you suspiciously when you entered the room—and John was uncharacteristically cheerful.

What's happening here?

For whatever reason, John appears to have named you as the source of some dissatisfaction in his work life. He's blamed you for that dissatisfaction, and is actively claiming something from you. In this case his claim—though negative and likely self-destructive—comes in the form of personal satisfaction.

Unless someone talks to John about his initial dissatisfaction, we'll never quite know why he began spreading rumors about you and creating ill feelings between you and your teammates. Still, we can make a few fair assumptions based on our knowledge of the social psychology of conflict.

There's perverse satisfaction to be gained by the chronically dissatisfied when they can make a drab day at the office momentarily dramatic, particularly when the drama includes exacting revenge from someone cast in the role of adversary. John's hallmark characteristic is a lack of control. He's disorganized, chaotic, impulsive, and unproductive. When he's able to create an atmosphere of suspicion about you, he's momentarily achieved the thing he most lacks, the thing you appear to have, the thing he believes people like you have deprived him of—control.

Though you needn't pity the poor Drama Queen, when you know what drives his difficult behavior, you have some chance of engaging him in a productive conversation about it. Productive conversation openers include, "How can I help you achieve the best outcome for you at the same time as we get the team's job done as best we can?" or "I've noticed your workload seems disproportionate to the time you have to devote to it. Is there something I can do to help lessen your burden?" More focused conversations about team morale could be commenced by noting that the spirit of the workplace is suffering and by asking John what he believes might be a good solution.

> *"Listen to his answers without judgment, and enlist his aid in solving the problem that has been impeding his efforts and your own."*

Any question that does not suggest blame and asks for an open-ended narrative response will lead to disclosures that will eventually identify the source of the problem. Communicate your faith in John, and in yourself, to resolve any problem the workplace gives rise to. Listen to his answers without judgment, and enlist his aid in solving the problem that has been impeding his efforts and your own. The former Drama Queen will hang up his pageant ribbon for renewed respect and creativity as a productive team member in no time.

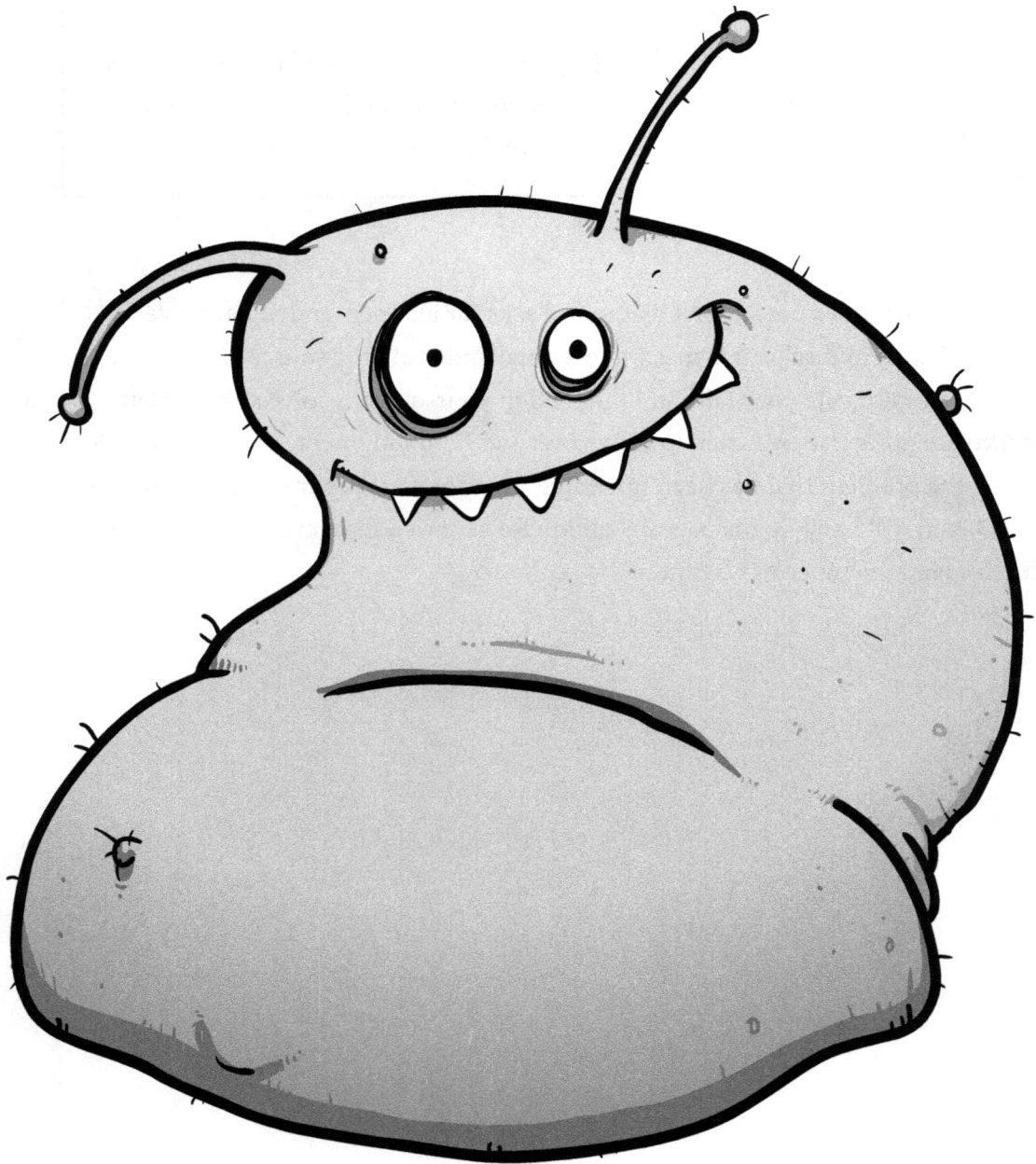

E

E is for Enemy

This is your enemy. He opposes that which you support, is hostile to those with whom you are friendly, seeks to destroy that which you have created, sows dissent where you seek consensus, and stands against every principle in which you believe.

Though some enemies are real (Japan bombing Pearl Harbor, or al-Qaeda terrorists flying passenger jets into New York's Twin Towers), others are imagined. As a nation, our imagined enemies have included people of nearly every color, creed, national origin, disability, political persuasion, and sexual preference. We have feared immigrants from Germany, Japan, Ireland, Italy, Iran, Mexico, and Puerto Rico, to name a few. We have also feared members of other religions—Jews, Catholics, and Muslims.

When our own countrymen formed groups ideologically opposed to the existing power structure, we feared them as enemies of the state—communists, socialists, and anarchists; free speech advocates, hippies, yippies, and weathermen; trade unionists and abolitionists; civil rights activists and women who sought the vote.

Entire nations have been our enemies. The former U.S.S.R. was our most visible national enemy for the second half of the twentieth century, even though our cold war never turned hot except by proxy. The last war supported by a majority of our country's citizens, World War II, was against enemies who are now our allies— Germany, Japan, and Italy.

Who we are matters deeply when we identify enemies. Europeans were enemies to the Native Americans, whose lands they invaded and occupied. The Portuguese, Dutch, English, Spanish, and French were enemies to the Africans who were captured and shipped as slaves to the new world. Before the civil rights movements of the mid- to late-twentieth century, American whites became the enemies of American blacks, and blacks of whites in America—a conflict that continues to resist our attempts to resolve it to this very day.

If you take a quick look in the mirror, odds are better than even that you'll see a present or former enemy of the United States looking right back at you.

With or without a reasonable basis to distrust and demonize others, we will do so anyway, creating in- and out-groups with remarkable ease and rapidity. Children and teenagers naturally divide themselves up by beauty, physical prowess or charm (popular kids); by interests such as music, theater or the visual arts; by clothes and grooming (goth, punk, or hippie kids); or by the use of alcohol or drugs (party kids and stoners). We use these identifiers (jocks, stoners, and the like) as cognitive shortcuts to quickly identify people who are likely to be friendly, loyal, and comprehensible without much study. They are our "homies"—our gangs or tribes. When we grow up, they become members of our political parties, churches, and occupations. More perniciously, they become our genders, our sexual preferences, and the colors of our skin.

The benefits of in-groups are many—community, safety, expansion of opportunity, friendship, and the sharing of work and resources. The detriments are also many. Once we become identified with one or more groups, we tend to view outsiders with suspicion and distrust, even hostility. To maintain a positive image of ourselves and our own in-group members (Christians, Americans, or even simply Pittsburgh Steeler fans) we tend to ignore our own shortcomings or misdeeds while emphasizing the negative traits of others. When misfortune befalls us and fortune favors them, we often fall into the naming, blaming, and claiming behavior that gives rise to active disputes and expresses itself in stereotyping and scapegoating. Professor, author, mediator and attorney, Dr. Kenneth Cloke, lists the eight steps people take to reduce a three-dimensional individual to a stereotype.

1. *Pick a characteristic*
2. *Blow it completely out of proportion*
3. *Collapse the whole person into the characteristic*
4. *Ignore individual differences and variations*
5. *Ignore subtleties and complexities*
6. *Ignore our common humanity*
7. *Make it match your own worst fears*
8. *Make it cruel*

Cloke, *Conflict Revolution, Mediating Evil, War, Injustice and Terrorism*

Our tendency to vilify, dehumanize, scapegoat, and murder out-group enemies is so well established that taking the steps necessary to avoid its disastrous effects is one of our most critical human projects. Fortunately,

> *"Fortunately, the best available treatment is the simple act of conversation."*

the best available treatment is the simple act of conversation. That which we have in common almost always exceeds that which divides us. We all seek shelter against the cold, food to ease our hunger, and companions with whom to share our joys and sadness, our hopes and dreams, our good times and bad. We all want to create a better world for our children and to protect them against harm. We all want to worship in the manner of our choosing, and to pursue work that satisfies our intellect and spirit.

The next time you see someone who has become your enemy, take time out to share food and drink. Ask that person how his journey is progressing, how his family is faring, what challenges he's facing, and how he's meeting those challenges. If we lead with our differences and value our own opinions over those of our fellows, we will generally find much about which to argue. Our differences divide us, and our opinions are assailable. If we lead with the story of our families and ourselves within them, the challenges we have faced and overcome, our dreams for the future, and the legacy we wish to leave for our children, there is little to assail and nothing about which to argue. When we have learned what the others think and feel, we no longer need to speculate about their motives, nor fear their foreign ways. Share of yourself and allow others to share with you. Your friends will be many and your enemies few.

F

F is for Friend

My Twitter account tells me I have more than two thousand "followers," and my Facebook page suggests I add someone new to my account as a "friend" nearly every day.

Despite our modern online age, people do not become friends, or loyal followers, at the push of a button. We start friendships tentatively, with small admissions of fallibility that won't entirely rip away the costume of the person we're pretending to be.

"I'm actually shy," I may tell an acquaintance. "The bravado masks it."

I pause and wait for a reciprocal revelation signaling a common desire to take the relationship in a more intimate direction—one in which I signal my willingness to be trusting and demonstrate my ability to be trusted.

"Me, too," my potential friend might acknowledge. "I'm actually driven by fear. I know I seem confident, but all this apparent success makes me feel like a fraud. Worse, I'm always feeling guilty that I'm not a better, more attentive mother to my children, because I'm so busy pursuing my own success. That's selfish, don't you think?"

With this response, my acquaintance is not only reciprocating our growing intimacy, she is deepening it. I was merely talking about my professional life. She's now drilled down into her relationship with her children. We are taking baby steps to friendship, testing one another's ability to move beyond our public selves and open up the door to our private lives and secret fears. We are putting something of ourselves on the line—something vulnerable and valuable—in the hope of finding another person who knows and cares about us—warts and all.

When you consider how vitally important friends are to our emotional well-being, it's surprising we don't have more friendship owners' manuals or, for that matter, friendship counseling. Bookstores are filled with advice manuals for marriages and parenting, but few titles advise us on the care and feeding of our friends—people who outlast marriages and endure long past the time our children leave home.

What happens when friendships go bad? And what, if anything, should we be doing to tend our friendship garden?

I made a new friend in school a few years ago. Our intimacy was forged in our mutual mid-life career crises at the Straus Institute in Malibu. We'd both decided to earn legal graduate degrees in dispute resolution with the intention of becoming mediators. Rod and I became friends for the same set of obvious and mysterious reasons that people fall in love. We were engaged in an activity that threatened to throw our well-ordered lives into turmoil, but which deeply engaged and challenged both of us. We were surrounded by law students who were decades younger than we were, were being taught by people who often had much less real-world experience than we did, and were understandably anxious about our decision to throw a couple of perfectly decent occupations out the window.

Just like any romance, my friendship with Rod had a honeymoon period. There was that small stretch of time during which we searched for and identified everything we had in common, reveling in our compatibility, and ignoring the quite obvious differences and potential conflicts that might arise between us. Rod was conservative in dress and manner, for instance, while I was far less restrained. Though not many years older, Rod's age put him on the other side of the profound cultural shifts of the late 1960s and early 1970s. I was in high school during the Summer of Love and in college when the women's movement took the country by storm. Rod was already married during those years, raising children while I was raising Cain.

Like the first lover's quarrel, friendships also have their early disputes. I wasn't, however, expecting so devastating a breach as the one that arrived early one spring morning.

Rod's and my master's program required us to spend a significant amount of time interning with local judges, arbitrators, or mediators. We'd met a local Superior Court judge at Straus whom we both liked. We secured permission to work with him as a team and showed up in his chambers in downtown Los Angeles.

Judge Jones was smart, voluble, and funny. I felt completely relaxed in his presence. It was there, in the judge's chambers, that I'd apparently used a word that my eighty-six-year-old mother was still trying to remove from my salty trial lawyer's vocabulary.

"F***!"

There are so many ways to use this word that I cannot recall how I used it on that occasion. "It was f***ing awesome," I might have exclaimed, or, "I can't f***ing believe it."

Weeks later, Rod called me at home, prefacing his remarks with words no one wants to hear—"I need to talk to you about something." This phrase is never followed by, "Let's have dinner," or "I have tickets to a concert. Would you like to join me?" I stiffened in my chair, took a deep breath, and said, "OK."

"I don't think I can continue to be associated with you," Rod said.

I remember the word "associated," because it stung. I've behaved badly from time to time, really badly, but no one ever told me they didn't want to be associated with me before. Tears sprung into my eyes.

"Because?" I asked.

"Because you said f*** in Judge Jones' chambers. I just can't allow myself to be affiliated with anyone who behaves in such an unprofessional manner. You've been in this legal community for more than two decades, but I haven't. I'm just establishing my reputation, and I don't think I can be building it if I'm associated with you."

I could have said, "Fine. It makes no difference to me one way or the other." That would have cut the conversation—and the relationship—off immediately. I could have—and in most circumstances likely would have—responded that way, but Rod and I were studying conflict resolution, for goodness' sake, and I valued his friendship despite—or maybe because of—the fact that it was so new for both of us. He made me laugh at myself when I was being overly earnest. He reminded me of my good qualities when I was feeling insecure. And he was the only person I knew who was willing to talk for hours about the intersection of the social psychology of conflict with the adversarial legal system. It would be a real loss if our newfound friendship suddenly disintegrated.

> *"From the time we're two or three years old, our instinct is to repair a loving relationship, not to terminate it."*

As my husband circled my chair trying to intuit why tears were streaming down my face, I asked Rod if he'd be willing to talk about the reasons my use of the word f*** disturbed him so much. "Was my behavior really so unforgivable that it's worth throwing our entire friendship away?"

In this moment, Rod and I were experiencing the first rupture in our relationship. I didn't just feel unhappy, I felt ashamed. Were I a toddler, shamed by my mother for running out into the street only to be snatched out of harm's way at the last moment, I would have done what all toddlers instinctively do—I would have physically reached out for affection in an effort to restore the bond between us and to repair the rupture.

Think about that for a moment. From the time we're two or three years old, our instinct is to *repair* a loving relationship, not to terminate it. This response is universal and natural. Only later will we learn to respond to disappointments in relationships with anger and withdrawal. Psychologists tell us that it is this process of rupture and repair that makes us flexible and adaptable. It helps us trust others to be reliable, and it permits us to form and maintain intimate relationships. It's what allows us to take risks with our emotions.

The toddler who seeks to repair the momentarily broken bond with his caregiver is also engaged in a process referred to as "self-righting." When parents respond lovingly, they help their child to return to a normal emotional and relational state—one in which love and trust is greater than disappointment and betrayal. This is what I was attempting to do with Rod. I wasn't defending my right to use the word f*** in the presence of the judge; I was attempting to affirm my belief that our disagreement was reparable and our friendship reliable. I was also attempting to right myself from the sudden shock and shame arising from such strongly expressed disapproval.

Many of us react to shaming with anger. This is not surprising, because shame is such a painful experience that it interferes with our sense of who we are, including the belief that we are competent, sensible, caring, reasonable people. When shame endangers our sense of self, anger helps us consolidate our experience and regain the self-regard necessary to live comfortably with ourselves and with others. Those who do not respond to shame with anger often simply withdraw, cutting off the shame-giver in an attempt to eliminate the shame. The healthiest among us can self-right by recalling that *who we are* is not *what we do*. When we are able to separate our sense of self from the way in which we behave, we tend to respond to shameful circumstances by acknowledging our wrong-doing, apologizing for it, making amends, and seeking reconciliation.

I'd learned some of these things in the course of my dispute resolution studies and I didn't want to take the course of anger or withdrawal. Even though I felt hurt and angry, I summoned up the small degree of courage necessary to take responsibility for behavior that I had to admit might offend many reasonable people. I apologized for embarrassing Rod in front of the judge, and I assured him that I was willing to drop the F-word from my vocabulary if it would save our friendship. In doing so, I was not only saying, "I'm sorry," I was letting Rod know that our friendship was important enough for me to sacrifice something of myself for.

In response, Rod admitted that he'd always been a bit of an old fogey. He told me that he genuinely liked and respected me. I could say f*** all I wanted, he said and laughed. I assured him that it was no shame to him to feel embarrassed by its use in a judge's chambers. We were both reaching beyond our ordinary limits to repair the break we'd just experienced.

In this manner, our friendship made it past its first challenge. Like a bone that has been broken and healed, the connection between us was strengthened. We not only assured ourselves of the continued benefit of one another's friendship, we proved our willingness to move past our own pride and self-interests to make peace in the face of discord. Though Rod has since moved to another part of the country, we remain good friends to this day.

Friendship, like romantic love, goes bad when we're unable to recover from the disappointment we feel when the rubber of our idealized image hits the road of our fallible human nature. If we choose to respond to these small crises with anger or withdrawal, we never learn how resilient we are and how reliable we can make our most important relationships.

In the *ABCs of Conflict Resolution*, F is not only for Friend, it also stands for fixing and forgiveness. It represents fallibility and the fearlessness that friendship sometimes requires. In my relationship with Rod, it stood for all of these things. And to the delight of my mother, it never again stood for f***.

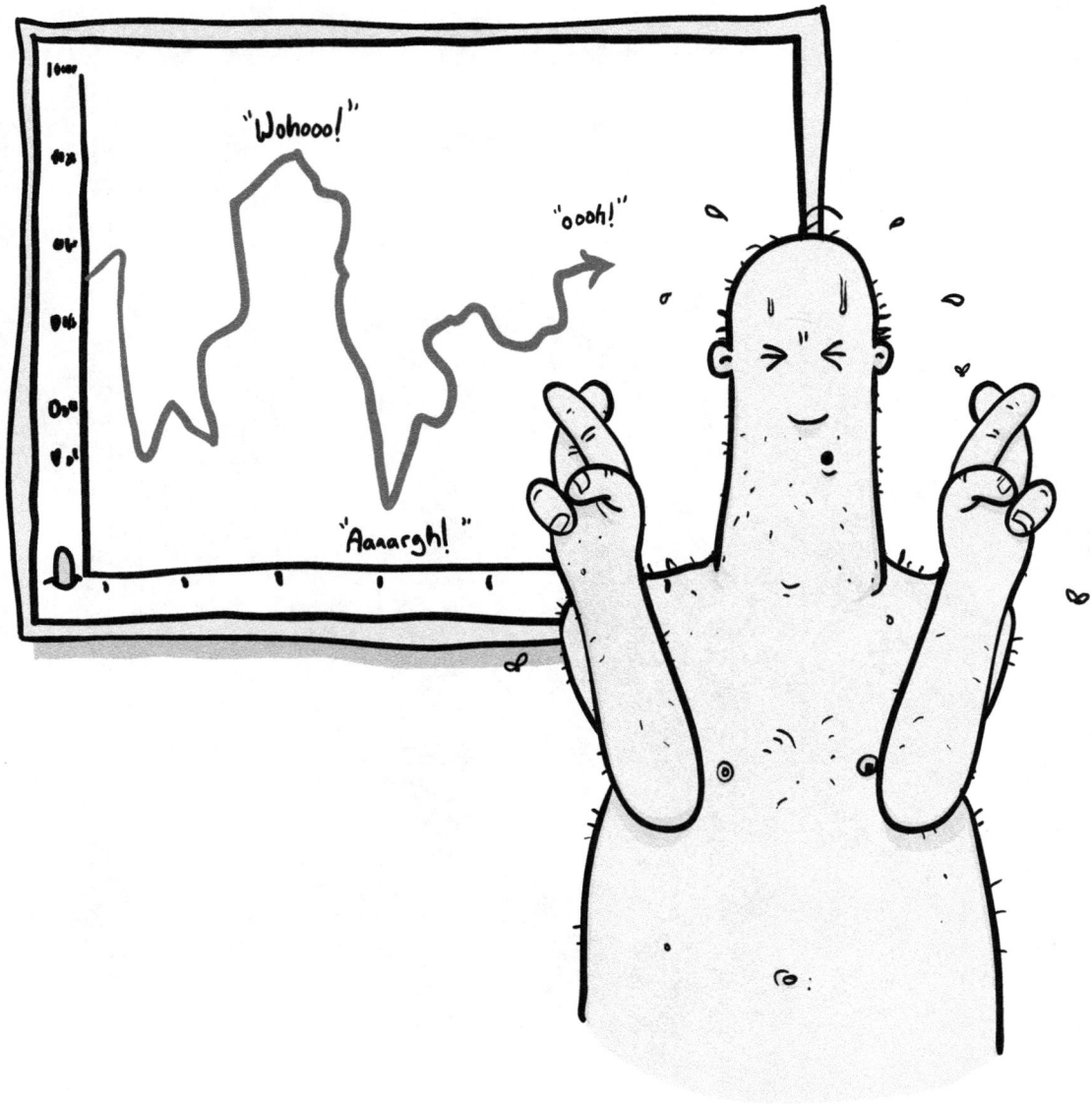

G

G is for Gambler

Whether we think so or not, we are all gamblers. Every day we place bets on the future of our families, our communities, and our nation. Heck, every time we step into our cars and turn the key in the ignition, we are betting that we will beat the traffic accident statistics, not to mention avoid the devastating effects of global warming. We invest in real estate or the stock market even as we see both of them heading south. We ask for a raise in a down economy, betting our self-esteem against the chance that we'll be better paid. We take a risk by moving into a neighborhood where the school system is sub-standard, believing that the neighborhood's gentrification will improve the local schools. We date, we get engaged, and we marry— we bet our lives on these intimate personal choices. He will be a good father and she a reliable economic partner. We will make a good team and raise a loving family.

Can we turn gamble into rational decision? And are our chances improved by following the dictates of our education rather than consulting our "gut" feelings? To learn the answer to these critical questions, we travel back in time to 1848, to the day a stick of dynamite blew up in Phineas Gage's face.

Gage was railroad man, busily tamping gunpowder into a stick of dynamite one moment and walking around with a three-foot metal rod through his head the next. It's the walking part that was so astonishing, as was Gage's nearly complete recovery, only a few months later. We remember Gage today, however, not for the bizarre nature of the accident, but for the workings of our minds that Gage's misfortune revealed.

In a rational age, Gage achieved what some might call perfection—he lost the part of his brain that gave him emotion. He was a purely rational man. Scientists of the day assumed that Gage would be enabled to make lightening fast decisions in the absence of interference with those pesky emotions—fear of failure, grief over lost opportunities, or even joy, which too often accompanies the rash and impulsive decision. As it happened, the perfectly rational man is incapable of making any decision whatsoever. Gage could make endless lists of pros and cons, but could no longer rely on his "gut" feelings to toss the list aside and choose.

More than one hundred years later, neuroscientist António Damásio used the story of Gage's post-accident personality changes, along with his own observations of brain-damaged patients, to conclude that no one makes purely rational choices. Far from interfering with decision-making, Damásio argued, emotion is what enables us to make up our minds.

Other neuroscientists followed Damásio's research with their own studies, all of which identify a Goldilocks Zone of emotive-rational decision-making. Too much emotion and too little information hamper us from making clear-eyed decisions about our future. On the other hand, too little emotion and too much thinking paralyze our decision-making process, preventing us from choosing one path over the other. It turns out that the neurochemical, dopamine, not only brings us pleasure, but also helps the brain find patterns that suggest probable outcomes. With just the right amount of this natural feel-good serum, we happily list the many rational reasons why we might actually win at one of the hundreds of slot machines. If someone else abandons their slot machine after an hour of play, we tell ourselves that it must be primed to pay off. With slot machines, as with much of life's experiences, there is no pattern from which we might profitably predict the future.

Still, in the absence of patterns, we will simply make some up. Nearby machines are paying off so this one should do so soon. It's a lucky day and a lucky machine because both carry the numbers of our birth. On and on

> *"Gather facts and figures, test your assumptions with people you trust, and listen as much to your rational mind as you do to your gut."*

we rationalize until our quarters are gone and we head back to our rooms angry with ourselves or with the gods of chance.

If we make up patterns when life makes no sense to us, and if we are susceptible to neurochemical reward and punishment, how can we be expected to make thoughtful decisions when faced with conflict—such as a deteriorating marriage, a willfull teen, or a bullying employer? The social scientists who study decision-making suggest finding the Goldilocks Zone. Gather facts and figures, test your assumptions with people you trust, and listen as much to your rational mind as you do to your gut. Proceed with caution when your brain is saying "Go, go, go," but your gut is saying, "No, no, no."

Because we're all gambling our lives against an unknowable future, the best we can do is to engage both our heads and our hearts when making decisions that will result in real consequences tomorrow. Be sufficiently wary of others to explore their bona fides, and trust your instincts even when you can't find a purely rational reason to do so, always remembering that your best hedge against uncertainty is the presence of friends and family members who consider your well-being to be of as much concern as their own.

H

H is for Hero

It was an unusually clear and sunny Tuesday morning in September when Thomas Burnett Jr., senior vice president and chief operating officer of a medical research company, boarded a plane in Newark, New Jersey heading for his home in the San Francisco Bay Area. Easing into his first-class seat as he accepted a glass of orange juice from the flight attendant, he nodded good morning to his row partner, Mark Bennett. Settling in for the five-hour flight, Thomas opened the front page of the *New York Times*—the early edition of the paper dated September 11, 2001.

Though Thomas and thirty-nine of his fellow passengers were headed for the West Coast, four others on Flight 93 had a different destination in mind. Ziad Jarrah, a Lebanese national, and three Saudi Arabians, Ahmed al-Haznawi, Ahmed al-Nami and Saeed al-Ghamdi, were poised to launch one of the boldest terrorist attacks ever undertaken on American soil. Jarrah, al-Haznawi, al-Nami, and al-Ghamdi—members of the little-known al-Qaeda terrorist network—intended not only to hijack this passenger plane, but to use it as a missile aimed at the heart America's political life— the White House or the US Capitol building.

At approximately the same time that Burnett and Bennett boarded Flight 93, fifteen al-Qaeda conspirators boarded three other flights—ttwo from JFK International in New York City and one from Logan Airport in Boston. They would hijack those flights, take over the planes' controls, and crash them into the Pentagon and New York City's Twin Towers, catapulting America into two actual wars (in Iraq and Afghanistan) and a metaphoric one—the War on Terror.

Just as it takes more than one person to be an asshole, a bully, or a coward, it takes more than one person to be a hero. There are no heroes without villains and no villains without victims. The villains in this tale were members of a group dedicated to winning a "war" their leader—Osama bin Laden—had declared against the United States in 1997. The intended victims of Flight 93 were neither its passengers nor its crew. The intended victim was the *idea of America*. To understand why men risk their lives for the love of their country, for honor, and for the lives of others, we must first turn back our evolutionary clock.

It's a picture-perfect morning in Eden, with the African veldt in full bloom. The small game has disappeared for reasons no one can fathom and all the low-hanging fruit was long ago picked and eaten. The children are hungry. Eve needs to find a new grove of trees or dig for some tubers in some other part of the valley. On this particular morning she's caring not only for her own five children but four of her sister's as well. Eve urges the young ones out of the village along a well-worn path, and then into uncharted territory.

As the day ends and dusk turns the valley a light blue-black, Eve is feeling good. She has gathered enough for her entire extended family and hasn't heard the sound of a predator all day. The children have played quietly in a copse of dense trees and underbrush all day long. She's only yards away from her well-behaved brood when she hears a crackling of twigs in the near distance. It is the tiger the cave paintings have warned her about. She has two choices—freeze in the hope that she hasn't yet been detected, or run for safety. There's a tall tree she could climb in the copse where the children are hiding, but if she runs in that direction, she will bring death right to them.

Eve doesn't have time to think about what she should do. She hasn't been schooled in ethics or raised with religious precepts. She hasn't yet developed the higher cognitive brain functions that require the weighing of responsibilities against self-interest. What spontaneous reaction will ensure that Eve's genetic material is passed along to future generations? Screaming out a warning to the children hiding in the bushes will bring the tiger directly to her, all but ensuring her death. In evolution's calculus, the survival of nine children carrying the same DNA gives that DNA a far better chance of appearing in future generations than does the survival of a single family member. Because Eve is pre-disposed to act in favor of the children, she reflexively screams out a warning, permitting nine DNA-carriers to survive another day. Those members of the tribe who do not act for the benefit of their family are less likely to have their genetic pre-dispositions passed along to future generations. And so it is, say the evolutionary biologists, that evolution has favored not simply the fittest individual, but the altruistic family member as well.

Tom Burnett and the other passengers on Flight 93 were not required to respond reflexively to the terrorist threat that faced them that September morning. They had time to think and to gather information from friends and family on the ground. Though we'll never know exactly what happened, journalists have pieced together a story based upon telephone conversations between the passengers and their loved ones.

Burnett placed several calls from the doomed airplane that day. He and his fellow passengers learned that three other planes had been hijacked, two of which had been flown into New York City's Twin Towers and one of which had crashed into the Pentagon. Burnett told his wife that passengers of Flight 93 were "going to do something" about their predicament, even as she tried to talk him out of taking any action.

"If they're going to crash the plane into the ground," he told his wife, "we have to do something. We can't wait for the authorities. We have to do something now."

That something was storming the cockpit. One family member who remained connected by telephone to the events unfolding on Flight 93 remembers hearing these now-famous words:

"Are you guys ready? Let's roll."

Little more than an hour later, United Airlines confirmed that Flight 93 had crashed in an open field near Pittsburgh, Pennsylvania, instantly killing everyone on board. Because of the heroism of its passengers, the United States Capitol and the White House in Washington, D.C. stand unharmed today.

There are two explanations for this behavior—one scientific and one spiritual. The scientific evolutionary explanation is the story of Eve we've just heard. We are hard-wired to sacrifice our own interests— even our own lives—to save our family. The scientists call this the "kin selection" theory of human altruism. Student and popularizer of the world's religions, myths, and legends, Joseph Campbell, has a more spiritual explanation.

> *"Although we cannot predict the circumstances that might require us to behave as heroes, we can prepare ourselves to choose self-sacrifice over naked self-interest."*

"You and I," Campbell once explained to newsman Bill Moyers,

> are one . . . two aspects of the one life, and . . . our apparent separateness
> is but an effect of the way we experience forms under the conditions of space
> and time. Our true reality is in our identity and unity with all life. This
> is a metaphysical truth, which may become spontaneously realized under
> circumstances of crisis... [I]t is... the truth of your life. The hero is the one who
> has given his physical life to some order of realization of that truth... [I]n small
> ways you can see this happening every day, all the time, moving life in the world,
> people doing selfless things to and for each other.

Although we cannot predict the circumstances that might require us to behave as heroes, we can prepare ourselves to choose self-sacrifice over naked self-interest. The heroes of Flight 93 did not give their lives for the survival of their biological families. They gave their lives for an ideal—that all Americans are family. We can honor those heroes by considering all people everywhere to be part of our family and worthy of our sacrifice.

Our potential to transcend our differences in favor of mankind's survival is present every time we are given the opportunity to resolve conflict. When people share their stories, challenges, fears, and concerns with one another, they begin to view one another as fellow creatures on the planet, whatever their ethnic, religious, or national origins. When we share the narratives of our lives, accusations slip away and strident opinionating evaporates. Tales of adversity and economic uncertainty unspool. Narratives of loss and grief bring tears and then laughter. As the poet Galway Kinnell once wrote, if we write our own personal experience deeply enough, what we hear will be the voice of another creature on the planet speaking. If we practice listening to one another as family, the voice we hear will be our own.

I

I is for Idiot

This man is an idiot who happens to be your boss. This idiot, named Ivan, expects you to arrive at the office at nine a.m. sharp. His hours, however, are completely unpredictable. Sometimes he arrives at six a.m., leaving a pile of work for you when you arrive three hours later, wanting all of it done immediately. On other days, he doesn't wander into the office until past noon. By the time he shows up, you've been covering for him all morning, taking his telephone calls, making excuses, and telling white lies, preventing you from getting your own work done. Though you've never actually seen him do it, you strongly suspect that Ivan is the office refrigerator thief, eating your Healthy Choice frozen dinners and homemade sandwiches late at night when he has only the cleaning staff to keep him company.

Just yesterday, Ivan put you in a real jam. You're up for promotion—a promotion that will get you out from under Ivan's thumb. As Ivan has known for weeks—make that months—you had an important full-day client presentation and consultation scheduled yesterday. As Ivan also knew, you'd been staying late for months to put the presentation together. The Big Boss would be there, the one who would give the thumbs-up or thumbs-down to your promotion. It had to be right—no, it had to be more than right. It had to be perfect.

Every single day last week, Ivan created some fresh disaster that required you to clean up the mess before returning to your own work. Only when that was done could you give the final touches to your presentation. You didn't get more than four hours sleep any night last week and you worked the entire weekend. By yesterday, you were not only frazzled and exhausted, you'd woken up that morning with a one hundred and two-degree temperature, and your future hung in the balance.

So what's up with Ivan? Is he intentionally trying to derail your promotion? Is he stupid? Or lazy? Or both? Is there anything you could have done to prevent him from ruining your week?

Let's take a step back from your difficulties with this particular idiot to examine one of the cognitive biases that interfere most profoundly with our ability to understand our fellows. The term cognitive bias simply means a common error we all make in our

> *"The term cognitive bias simply means a common error we all make in our attempt to understand the actions and motives of others. "*

attempt to understand the actions and motives of others. Here's the cognitive bias that is the key to unlock the door labeled *what the heck is he thinking*?

That bias is known as "fundamental attribution error." The bias is fundamental because we all share it. The bias is one of attribution because it affects the way in which we attribute intention or circumstance to injury-causing behavior. The bias is error, because *we will always draw the wrong conclusion unless we are extremely attentive to the problem.*

Let's use Ivan as a means of exploring this bias. Ivan is erratic in his behavior and seemingly unconcerned with anyone's well-being but his own. You've likely concluded that Ivan is either incompetent or malicious. Though you may be right about Ivan, chances are that you are over-attributing intentionality to his actions and under-attributing circumstance. You, like everyone else on the planet, errs in this fashion for one very good reason—if another person's behavior is causing you harm, it is actually better for you if he is doing so "on purpose." Why? Because you have some chance of controlling the behavior of someone who is intentionally causing you harm.

Through anger, manipulation, contentious dispute resolution tactics, or retaliation, you have some hope of changing an intentional wrongdoer's behavior. He will be shamed into right action, scared into more civilized conduct, or even sufficiently enlightened to realize the error of his ways followed by attempts to right that which he has put wrong. That the wrongdoer will see the error in his ways or be too afraid to continue behaving in a harm-causing manner is the hope. In truth, you are making assumptions about Ivan's motives, even though you believe you have really good reasons for doing so. His behavior is causing you harm. If, as is equally likely, Ivan's erratic behavior is the result of circumstances beyond his own control, your chances of changing Ivan for the better is pretty slim indeed.

The corrective to fundamental attribution error, and the potential for resolving the Ivan problem, is a three-step process. First, you must remember that you, like everyone else, may well be over-ascribing intention to Ivan's office misbehavior. Second, you can ask Ivan whether his family or personal circumstances are responsible, at least in part, for his thoughtless treatment of his coworkers. I recall the chagrin that my fellow lawyers and I felt about a coworker who fell asleep at his desk after lunch every day. We exchanged gossip and said dreadful things about this man, including accusations that he was lazy, too old to still be practicing law (in his late 50's, my own age now), or drinking his lunches. What we eventually learned was that our colleague was suffering from leukemia and would pass away within the year. Had we bothered to ask him about his circumstances, the law firm would happily have adjusted his schedule to permit a time, and more comfortable place, for an afternoon rest. To our lasting shame, we secretly ridiculed and spread malicious gossip about a very sick man rather than helping him make the last months of his working life ones of value to him and to the firm.

The solution to fundamental attribution error, like the solution to many other biases, is to first recognize that we possess them. Taking action to accurately assess the situation can be as easy as asking a casual question in the coffee room.

"Hey, Ivan," you might say, "you're keeping a pretty erratic schedule that's making my own workload difficult to handle. You used to be so dependable. Has anything changed?"

"Well, yes," Ivan might confide. "My eight-year-old daughter was diagnosed with bone cancer six months ago. The doctors amputated her leg two months ago and we've been deeply involved in her physical therapy—getting a prosthetic leg and helping her learn how to use it. I didn't really want to tell anyone. It's so personal. And I'm worried about layoffs."

Now that you understand Ivan's purely personal and human reasons for his "misbehavior," you not only sympathize with his plight, you can begin a process of problem solving in which both your and Ivan's needs may well be met at the same time. Perhaps he needs a compassion leave from work while you retain a temporary worker to replace him until his daughter is better. Maybe you know about some social service resources that can get his daughter back and forth to her physical therapy appointments, relieving him of some of the burdens that are interfering with his job responsibilities. The potential remedies are as endless as the useful speculation in which we engage when we try to explain someone's circumstances by their behavior instead of going to the source and simply asking about it.

Conflict resolution pros combat cognitive biases by recognizing their pernicious effect, asking questions to diagnose conflict problems at home and in the workplace, and brain storming solutions in attempt to find a resolution that is best for everyone.

J

J is for Judge

Lawyers spend their professional lives trying to persuade judges that their clients are right and their opponents wrong. We do this, even though the truth generally lies in a gray area somewhere south of righteousness and north of certainty. Seeking out the assistance of a judge to determine the truth and apply the law comes naturally to us. It goes back to our earliest spats over pilfered blocks and rigged board games. As children we sought out the nearest authority figure who was almost always named Mom.

"Bobby slugged me," Judie says, her face streaked with tears as she points an accusing finger at her little brother.

"Did not!"

"Did so!"

Mom asks each child to tell the story of the event. "One at a time," she cautions when both children begin speaking at once. "Judie first," she says, unknowingly following the same rule a judge in a court of law would—allowing the injured party to present her case first.

"He hit me," Judie weeps. "Here, on my arm! He punched me, right in front of my friends! They can tell you what happened!"

Mom turns to the youngest. "Bobby?"

Bobby might deny the charge or justify it, just like any defendant would in a court of law.

"They wouldn't let me play with them," Bobby says, his eyes tearing up, too. "They said only girls could play house. Then Judie started calling me a sissy, and her friends did too. 'Bobby is a sissy, Bobby is a sissy!' they said. I shouted at them to stop, but they wouldn't, and then Judie called me a 'faggot.'"

By now you know the way in which conflict turns into disputes. Someone's been hurt. He searches the field for someone to name as the source of his harm, someone to blame for unfairly visiting injury upon him, and someone from whom to claim recompense. In this case, as in most legal actions, each party names the other as the source of the injury, finds a reason why the other's behavior is worthy of censure, blames the other, and makes a claim. If the house rules don't permit girls to exclude boys, Bobby has a legitimate gripe. Added to Bobby's claim of unfair exclusion is his contention that he's suffered emotional harm as a result of name-calling and taunting by his sister and her friends.

Instead of running to Mom to resolve the dispute, Bobby took things into his own hands and resorted to the most primitive of conflict-resolution methods, violence, a dispute resolution tactic permissible in law only if one's own physical well-being is endangered. Even then, the violent physical response must be *proportional* to the threatened harm. Both the law and Mom say, "two wrongs don't make a right." Bobby's reaction won't necessarily take the heat off Judie. Taunting may be discouraged, but most mothers would apply the folk rule that we've all got to have a bit of a tough skin to make it in the world. You know the phrase from childhood: "Sticks and stones may break my bones, but words will never hurt me."

If Mom acts as the judge, as most parents do, she will likely punish Judie for rule-breaking and name-calling and discipline Bobby for hitting his sister. Mom, like a judge and jury, will not simply apply rules of law (no hitting, no teasing, no deprivation of game privileges based upon gender roles) to the facts as she finds them, she will consider the circumstance in which the fighting broke out in the first place as well as the gravity of the harm caused to both parties and the intentionality of the wrongdoing. If the reported facts differ—if, for instance, Bobby denies having hit Judie —Mom will either seek the testimony of eyewitnesses (Did Judie's friends see Bobby hit her? Can Judie please ask her friends to come and tell what really happened?) or cross-examine both parties, probing their stories for inconsistencies and pressing them for motives—why, for instance, Judie would lie about Bobby hitting her? Mom, like a judge, might also ask to see physical evidence. Is Judie's arm bruised? Can Bobby —who admits to having spent the entire day in Judie's physical presence—explain how the bruise on Judie's arm got there?

Eventually Mom will decide whom she believes, and the seriousness of each party's crime against the other. She will give her judgment and mete out her punishment. She is the judge of first and last resort. There is no appeal from Mom, as there is from the decision of every trial judge in every court—state or federal—in the land.

Mom is an efficient, effective, and final resolver of her children's disputes. Because she knows and loves them, she applies empathy as well as kindness to their conflicts. When adults judge one another in a courtroom, it's an entirely different story, even if the rules are similar. The dispute resolved in Court often won't look much like the conflict the parties brought to their lawyers in the first place. It settles only legal matters, not the personal issues, and few of the fairness problems that made the parties seek out the aid of the justice system in the first place.

Like the author Anne LaMott in her brilliant guide to writers, *Bird by Bird*, we are all hoping for a "justice acre" all our own. "You get one," writes LaMott,

> *your awful Uncle Phil gets one, I get one... everyone gets one. And as long as you don't hurt anyone, you really get to do with your acre as you please. You can plant fruit trees, or flowers, or alphabetized rows of vegetables, or nothing at all. If you want your acre to look like a giant garage sale or an auto-wrecking yard, that's what you get to do with it. There's a fence around your acre, though, with a gate, and if people keep coming into your land and sliming it or trying to get you to do what they think is right, you get to ask them to leave. And they have to go because this is your acre.*

We don't, however, live only on our own private justice acre. We live, work, play, tussle, share, petition, exhort, inspire, bully, and praise one another in the public justice acres that belong to everyone. With most of the rules we follow, there are the folk rules we learn as children—say please and thank you; first in time, first in right; help the elderly and disabled; share with your siblings; don't shove; always do your best. The other rules—the ones that

> *"Judges are the stick when we cannot get along or do the right thing."*

form the absolute boundaries of behavior in the public square—are the criminal laws initially enforced by sheriffs and police and the civil laws primarily enforced by judges and juries. It is only because we have such rules of law, and a robust justice system to enforce them, that the weakest citizen is protected from outlaws and bullies and the strongest government is restrained from interfering with all citizens' most basic rights.

The *ABCs of Conflict* takes pride in our system of justice, even as we recommend the resolution of most disputes through cooperative decision-making and problem solving. Judges are the stick when we cannot get along or do the right thing. The legal boundaries are both the limits of permissible behavior and the protective ring surrounding us all. The rule of law prevents the tyranny of our rulers and the anarchy of the mob. For the enforcement of the rule of law, we need impartial justice and procedural due process—notice that someone is seeking recompense in a court of law and an opportunity to be heard in that court before any negative sanction is imposed upon us. To help us anticipate the future consequences of our actions today, our courts follow precedent—legal rules developed in the course of adjudicating the rights and remedies of our citizens when they have had disputes that are similar to our own. The courts must be firm but fair, dependable but flexible. And for all our complaints, the court system does a pretty darn good job of this every working day.

As an initial threat to bring your adversary to the negotiation table, or as a last resort when negotiations fail, no society has yet to think of any better institution to keep public order while at the same time assuring the greatest degree of freedom to those who seek its aid. Mom's wisdom, however, is more often found in the mediation room where the parties are asked to be accountable for their contribution to the dispute, to brainstorm ways to resolve the problem, to seek and grant forgiveness, to made amends to the other, and to reconcile those differences that require wise and understanding hearts as much or more than legal sharp minds. Both mediation and litigation are available to help you resolve those conflicts that baffle and enrage you. Choose well, choose wisely, and may your days pass in justice.

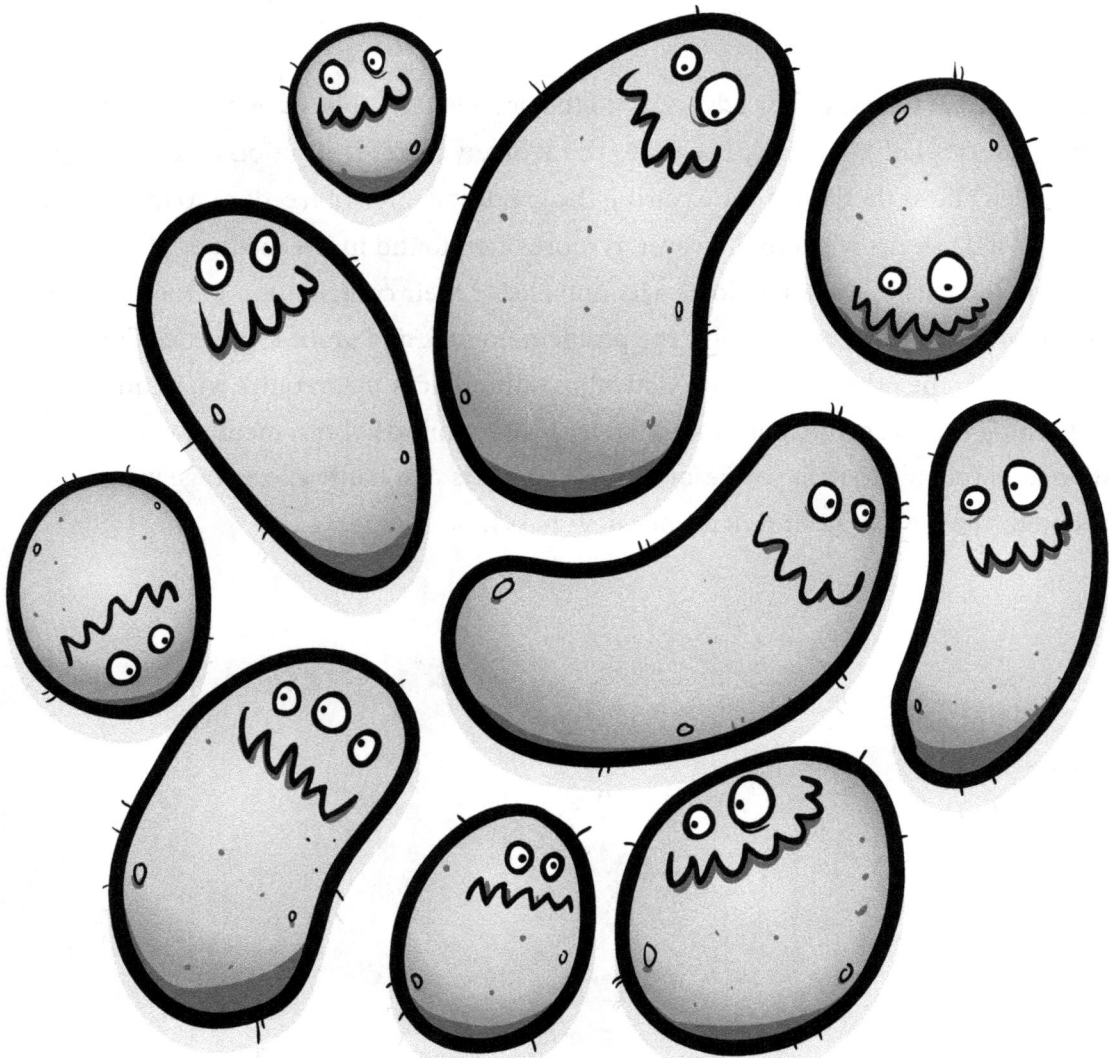

K

K is for Kin

In *What Every Person Should Know About War, New York Times* correspondent Chris Hedges estimates that between one hundred and fifty million to one billion of us have been killed in all the wars ever fought by humankind, one hundred and eight million of whom lost their lives in wars waged during our most civilized era, the twentieth century. Defining war as an active conflict in which more than one thousand people are killed, Hedges writes that we have been at peace for only two hundred and sixty-eight of our thirty-four hundred years of recorded history. That's eight percentage points of peace, folks—a dismal human record.

If a propensity for physical violence were the most prominent human characteristic, we surely would have wiped ourselves off the face of the earth by now. That we haven't speaks to something even deeper within us than our collective desire to dominate others and control all available resources for our own benefit. Let's take a deep breath and pause to remember that despite our sorry history of armed conflict, we also managed to land men on the moon, eradicate or drastically reduce a wide array of infectious diseases, end legalized racial segregation, grant women the right to vote in nearly every country in the world, and build civilizations that, for all their flaws, exhibit nearly continuous progress from barbarity to self-governance. At the local level, most of us stop at red lights, wait patiently in line at the grocery store, refrain from hitting one another when angry, stay off other people's property unless invited, play organized sports according to rules laid down decades ago, sit quietly through lectures, plays and movies, arrive at work on time, and pay for what we gather in retail stores to feed and clothe our families. In *extremis*, we not only behave ourselves, we often act heroically—putting our own lives in danger to save those of others—even when they are strangers to us. Firemen enter burning buildings, doctors and nurses risk their own health tending the well-being of others, police officers chase men with guns and enter abandoned buildings even when doing so is likely to get them injured or killed, and a great number of us would reflexively dash out into a street to save someone else's child from being run over by a truck.

If each of us has decided to answer to the higher angels of our human nature, how might we convince our fellows to do the same? In 1984, Professor Robert Axelrod issued a worldwide invitation seeking winning computer strategies for a game called the Prisoner's Dilemma. The Prisoner's Dilemma poses a problem involving trust, self-seeking, and collaboration that economists use to show why people so often fail to cooperate even when it is in their mutual best interests to do so.

The game begins its life as the story of a human dilemma. Two suspects are arrested by the police for burglary. Because the police do not have sufficient evidence to convict either suspect, they need at least one prisoner to confess and rat out his partner. To coax a confession from the miscreants, the police offer each person the same deal— if either one testifies against his partner, he will be freed and his partner will receive a ten-year sentence. If both confess and implicate the other, they will each receive a five-year sentence. If both remain silent, they will be sentenced to only six months in jail.

The optimal choice for both partners in crime is to cooperate with one another by remaining silent. If they do so, each will earn only a six-month jail sentence. The optimal solution for the individual suspect is to rat out his partner and secure his own freedom. Because neither partner is capable of predicting the other's choice, the only rational decision is mutual betrayal.

In real life, we play this game of cooperation or betrayal among the same group of people repeatedly. Recognizing that, Professor Axelrod asked entrants in his contest to devise a strategy for winning repeated rounds of the game—a version called the "iterated" Prisoners Dilemma for the number of iterations or "rounds" the game takes.

Of the fifty iterated Prisoner Dilemma programs submitted to Professor Axelrod, one was the clear winner, and its name was *Tit for Tat*. The *Tit for Tat* program began each round of play with cooperation. If cooperative play was met with betrayal, *Tit for Tat* retaliated on the next occasion it met the non-cooperative gamer. Only if the rogue program returned to cooperation would *Tit for Tat* do the same. Those programs that were designed to cooperate haphazardly or to continue cooperating in the face of betrayal, were repeatedly victimized. Those programs that chronically betrayed their fellow gamers became locked in escalating spirals of retaliatory play. Only *Tit for Tat* behaved the way evolutionary biologists believe successful human survivors played the game of life.

As we already saw in the chapter H is for Hero, evolutionary survivors are pre-disposed to cooperate with their fellows in at least some circumstances—those in which their family or kin are threatened. Because we're talking about only some circumstances, and an inclination rather than a universal response, not everyone will cooperate. We therefore need a means of bringing disreputable players back into the cooperative endeavors that account for our survival as a species after millions of years of pre-history. Unsurprisingly, that method is punishment. Banishment or penalties of death for non-cooperative players were options only under the most extreme circumstances. To survive, families needed all hands on deck. The fittest survivors punished proportionally and forgave quickly, as soon as a slap on the wrist brought uncooperative family members back into line.

We appear to be hard-wired for cooperation in the same way *Tit for Tat* was programmed for success. When research subjects played the iterated Prisoner's Dilemma while attached to equipment monitoring brain activity, the brains of those who were cooperating with one another lit up like pinball machines. Not only did the cooperators win more total points for cooperation than the betrayers, they were *happier* whether they were winning or not. As the neuroscientists discovered, when we cooperate, the neurochemical that gives us pleasure—dopamine—is released. At the same time that the cooperators' brains were being bathed in the warm glow of dopamine, their impulse inhibition areas were activated, helping them resist the lure of self-seeking.

> *"K is for Kin because the human family survives together, or not at all."*

Let's review. Our evolutionary history has created us to be a "band of brothers"— a human family that places the well-being of the tribe on a higher level than any one individual. If family members betray us (and they will) we doom our effort to secure compliance if we fail to retaliate. A sharp slap on the wrist or even expressed disapproval (the powerful shock of shaming) is usually sufficient to bring miscreants back into line. To optimize the benefits to be gained by cooperation among the greatest number of family members, we must be quick to forgive when our retaliatory actions bear fruit.

In the *ABCs of Conflict Resolution*, K is for Kin because the human family survives together, or not at all.

L

L is for Lawyer

One day toward the end of my first year of mediation practice, a much more experienced friend, Joe, asked me to mediate a will contest without the benefit of my usual "clergy"—lawyers with experience in the field. Our conversation went something like this:

Joe (Mediator): The family doesn't want to hire a lawyer. They just want to mediate.

Vickie: But I know absolutely nothing about wills, trusts, and estates. The parties need to talk to a lawyer first to learn their rights and remedies.

Joe: You still don't get it, do you?

Vickie: Get what?

Joe: It's not about rights and remedies. It's about interests.

Vickie: But how can they evaluate their interests without knowing their rights and remedies?

Joe: Because they're not interested in what the law says—they want to do what they believe is right for them as a family under the circumstances.

These people wanted to resolve a *legal dispute* without knowing their *legal rights?* Were they *nuts ?*

I understood "interests"—people's desires, needs, and preferences that could (and routinely do) erupt into disputes when unfairly frustrated or denied. These interests, along with people's fears, are what drive us to take legal positions. They are justification for our claim that we are legally entitled to recompense. Sometimes the interests that drive people and businesses to seek lawyers like me are non-economic – the desire for revenge; the need to hear people and businesses acknowledge that they caused us harm; our own fears of failure; the hope everyone has for forgiveness and reconciliation. But I'd been in the rights and remedies business for so long that I couldn't imagine people resolving disputes without a legal analysis. Weren't people's *interests* secondary to their *rights?* I was stubborn in my refusal to get it, until I recalled the divorce that ended my first marriage.

At that time I had refused advice from my attorney colleagues, insisting that I could handle the matter myself (a fool for a client). Why? Because community property laws didn't govern the marriage that took my husband through his graduate studies and me through law school.

No, we didn't have an enforceable pre-nuptial agreement, I told my legal mentors. Yes, I did realize I was entitled to half of our community property and to spousal support. So why wasn't I filing legal papers and making demands?

Because I wasn't interested in my legal rights. I had a *moral* obligation to abide by the agreement my husband and I had made from the start. When we met, he was already headed to graduate school and had saved enough money to pay his own way, as well as his living expenses. He'd get his degree while I worked to save the money necessary to pay for my legal education. Because our earning and spending habits were as different as could be, we agreed to keep our finances separate, on a monthly basis contributing an agreed-upon sum to a joint account for household and emergency expenses. This worked well for us. I indulged our pleasures and he saved his money. We were adults and we made decisions that carried consequences. We had a deal. There was no way I was going to break my word, even though I was experiencing the failure of my marriage.

Though well aware of my legal right to half our community property and to spousal support until my legal practice got off the ground, and though knowledgeable about the remedies available to me—monthly support payments for a limited period of time, plus a rough division of all marital assets—enforcing my rights simply didn't matter as much to me as keeping my promises. My interests—my highly personal desires, needs, values, and preferences—could be met without knowing anything whatsoever about the law.

I rented furniture and moved to a one-bedroom apartment in a low-income community in South Sacramento. I was poor again for a time—emotionally bereft, of course—but I hadn't added a legal dispute to my troubles. I felt as honorable as anyone ever can in severing a relationship. That relationship had contributed so much to the emotional strength I had needed at the time while preparing for, commencing, and completing law school, as well as starting my legal practice. I knew deep in my heart that during the years in which the marriage lasted, I could not have accomplished any of those goals without my husband's love and undeviating belief in my potential.

So I could, after all, understand why the family with the will dispute did not want legal advice, or the pressure of a rights and remedies analysis, to resolve their highly personal and entirely unique conflict. If they wanted to pursue and satisfy their idiosyncratic needs and desires, as well as to quell fears and live their values, they deserved a mediator who could help them do so without pestering them with a legal analysis.

The availability of mediation to settle disputes without lawyers does not diminish the importance of the rule of law governing the outer boundaries of acceptable behavior.

I support and defend with great ferocity the primacy of the rule of law in America. The causes of action, the denials and affirmative defenses, as well as the "facts" relevant to each, comprise a critical part of the dispute package that clients bring to lawyers for assistance. I haven't abandoned the rich tradition, heritage, and precedent of the law. What I have done is to expand my understanding of the conflicts every legal action presents. No longer constrained by "relevant" facts, I am able to open up the dispute to explore the "irrelevant" factors that ignited the conflict in the first place—the hurtful words or silences that flamed its embers and the activities that might reduce or even extinguish the conflagration.

I realize now, as I did when I divorced my husband, that "irrelevant" facts and principles sometimes run *contrary* to the law, and are often far more personally compelling. These irrelevancies often lie at the heart of a client's insistence to pursue litigation, of his decision that it is not worth further expense, or of his hesitancy to accept an offer rather than go to trial. These emotional responses and value choices are often the key that unlock the doors of resolution, not a barrier to the dispute's conclusion. As I sift through the relevant facts and applicable law, I am now more mindful of non-monetary interests—the strain litigation would place on my client, or the distraction it might be to more fruitful pursuits.

> *"For my own peace of mind, first I want to know my rights. Then I'll do what I think is right, regardless of them."*

Still, some wrongs demand legal redress, and wishing conflict away will not make it so. For my own peace of mind, first I want to know my rights. Then I'll do what I think is right, regardless of them.

M

M is for Mediator

That's me—a mediator. After twenty-five years of legal practice, waging battles with words in courts of law, I became what's known as a neutral—someone trained and skilled in helping people resolve their own disputes by facilitating dialogue, conversation, and negotiation between or among them. My own story of transformation from a competitive position-based adversarial lawyer to an interest-based, collaborative mediator begins in the suburbs of mid-century America, where it felt like the whole country was being invented just for me. Trucks lumbered through our neighborhood day after day, churning concrete or pouring tar. The air smelled of sawdust and the wind carried the high whine of band saws into my elementary school classroom.

Everyone's father was home from the war and building stuff—corrugated steel patio roofs, winding brick walkways, and freshly poured concrete drives. If you were lucky and had indulgent parents, you got to plunge your hands into the wet gray goo, leaving forever your unmistakable, one-of-a-kind, very own handprints on the back patio or garden walk. If you were very lucky, Dad—the world's greatest expert in everything—would let you use his tools.

To this day my all-time top-five favorite tools are the level, saw, hammer, trowel, and retractable tape measure. But really, it was the level I loved best. No skinned-knee girl ever took more pleasure in getting two little bubbles to float exactly side by side in their parallel glass vials than me.

"Eye to eye," said Dad, leaning over me in the hot sun as I pushed another brick into the wet cement. "You've got to get those bubbles eye to eye."

If I did that—got the bubbles eye to eye—that brick, and the next, and the one after that, would sit straight and true. You could build a whole wall in a single afternoon, until the air grew chilled, the outdoor lights clicked on, and Mom called everyone in for dinner. It was warm and bright at the kitchen table on those evenings, and everything outside the circle of our own small family was in perfect balance.

That was a child's perception, of course—a perception that preceded the shattering end in 1963 when a bleak November delivered our president in a flag-draped box while the television repeated, in endless slow motion, Oswald crumpling over Jack Ruby's gun.

Then they took King, too, bleeding on a Memphis balcony, and Bobby in the pantry of the Ambassador Hotel, home of the Coconut Grove—the old L.A. hotspot that mourns him still—shuttered and abandoned on Wilshire Boulevard. Relentlessly they picked our heroes off, one by one, and then sent half our generation to war as the other half fought against it.

Anger, say the psychologists, consolidates our sense of self when fear and certainty begin to break down our old ways of being. I didn't have to look far for companions in those days, all of whom were ready to throw down their own levels and take up hammers and saws. Marches, accusations, and invective followed. There were no cops, only fascist pigs; no America, only the military-industrial complex; no family, only a loose affiliation of like-minded idealists. And though I eventually left the counter-culture for law school, the apparatus of contention I learned there buried Dad's level even deeper in my toolbox.

After a quarter-century of high-stakes commercial litigation, I realized I had become the Queen of Conflict Escalation. In mid-career, searching for balance, I wanted a change. I first stumbled upon the Straus Institute for Dispute Resolution at Pepperdine University in a downtown hotel conference room, having enrolled in its *Mediating the Litigated Case* program. Entering the room, I saw a Gulliver-sized Post-it note on which was written a single, short phrase:

Be Conscious.

A Buddha's instruction. I was in the right place. Over the course of that forty-two-hour training session, I realized I wouldn't have to give up anything to mediate—certainly not the critical reasoning ability born in law school, or the contentious tactics. These Straus men and women were not hearts-and-flowers peaceniks.

At Straus, I found the tools of contention categorized and labeled—ingratiation, gamesmanship, shaming, promises, argumentation, threats, tit for tat, coercive commitments, and non-violent engagement. For those of us who still remember Word Perfect, taking dispute resolution courses at the Straus Institute was like hitting the "reveal codes" button on an otherwise pristine page of type. Little by little, I began to learn more deeply about that which, up to now, I had been practicing only on the surface.

The first simulation in which our instructors engaged us confirmed the value of playing the X card—Straus-ese for being responsively non-cooperative, for engaging in the age-old game of tit for tat. Firm boundaries and a slap on the wrist remained necessary for uncooperative participants. We could continue to ingratiate, to threaten, to promise, and to demand commitments. We just needed to be conscious of what we were doing and of the effect our escalating tactics would inevitably have.

As a mediator I had to pick up new tools, clumsily at first, still clinging to my hammer and saw when the going got rough. As a litigator, I had been required to deliberately silence my desire for human connection—to respond empathically to opposing counsel's complaint that he truly make an effort to respond appropriately to the discovery that is a litigator's stock in trade. As a mediator, I now sit in a room two or three times a week, holding Dad's level in my hand and keeping the Straus injunctions in mind—be comfortable with what I don't know; be flexible and intuitive in responding; listen to both sides with equal attentiveness and depth; find some part of myself, no matter how small, in each side.

> *"It is not easy to stop being an argumentative, reactive adversary and become an understanding, open-hearted-yet-still-tough-minded professional."*

This is the inner work—and work it is. It is not easy to stop being an argumentative, reactive adversary, and become an understanding, open-hearted-yet-still-tough-minded professional. Some part of me is always shouting my predispositions in my ear, asking me to cling to my own prejudices, the ones I hold dear, temporarily forgetting that every litigant is someone just like me—someone who shares my own character flaws, including self-interest, mild-to-serious paranoia, anger, and fear—someone who believes, like I still too-often do, that we can track down the one and only absolute truth and bring it to its knees, trembling in naked submission.

Now I've got the cement and a new load of bricks. I am stacking them carefully one by one, level in hand. I've acquired new friends and colleagues who are eager to lend a hand—even friends who are willing to suggest that I've unbalanced the whole structure once again.

And yet, a new neighborhood appears to be growing up around me again. I can smell the sawdust sometimes, carried up the hill to my new dispute resolution home on the back of a cool sea breeze.

N

N is for Neighbor

These are our neighbors, the Coopers. My husband and I don't know them very well even though they live next to us on a cozy Los Angeles residential street. We know that Ron teaches Spanish at a local university and that his wife, Rochelle, formerly a talent agent, has been out of work for some time. We hear their eight-year-old son perfecting his basketball moves on Saturday mornings. We don't need to set our alarm clock in the morning because the Coopers' dog, Popeye, begins barking every day at six thirty a.m. Natalie, their youngest, is walking now, and we hear her older brother taking advantage of her in the way some siblings do.

Recently we saw a realtor pounding a *For Sale* sign into the Cooper's front yard. Our neighbors to the north, who hear more gossip than we do, tell us that Rochelle has concluded she'll never work in the entertainment business again. It seems she has returned to school to become a therapist. It also appears as if the family may be facing foreclosure.

If we lived in another country, or if we all belonged to a single religious group, we might come together to help the Coopers save their house. But we don't. We express sympathy when we discuss our neighbors' plight. "It will be hard for the kids," we predict, walking past their house on our way to the shopping mall. "Ron and Rochelle did such a great job with the front yard, it would be a shame for them to lose their equity."

Our sympathy does not lead us to trump our own self-interest in favor of the interests of our neighbors. Is that because we're thinking with our heads instead of our hearts? Not according to social scientists. We're actually more generous when we *think* our way into "right action" than when we *feel* our way into "right emotion." Perspective-taking, we're told, requires us to understand and anticipate the interests, thoughts, or likely behaviors of our neighbors. Empathy or sympathy, on the other hand, requires us to have compassion for others.

To test whether thinking leads to better collaborative outcomes than feeling, researchers designed three studies. In two of them, the participants negotiated the sale of a gas station, where a deal based solely on price was impossible because the seller's asking price was higher than the buyer's limit. Because both parties' underlying interests were compatible, however, creative deals were possible. In the first study, those participants who scored high on the perspective-taking portion of a personality inventory were more likely to successfully reach a deal. Here's the big surprise. The participants who scored higher on empathy were less successful than their perspective-taking peers in reaching a creative and collaborative agreement.

It turns out that the key to reaching creative negotiated agreements is not empathy, but the ability to recognize that our own interests are the same or similar to the interests of our bargaining partners. We feel sorry for the Coopers (empathy) but have no reason to ask them any questions that might reveal that *their* problem might be *our* problem as well. It's under circumstances like these where a bit of conflict might be good for everyone.

Let's assume that we learn the Coopers are on the verge of selling their house to a local fraternity. *Now* we have a conflict. As scenes of drunken college kids playing ear-shattering music at three a.m. begin to play out in our minds, we'd quickly begin to search for solutions to the looming neighborhood problem. Over the garden fence, my husband, a lawyer, might suggest to our neighbor, the satellite engineer, that we might be able to obtain an injunction from the court prohibiting the use of the Coopers' property as a fraternity house. The local zoning laws might give us the *right* to prevent the sale, but lawsuits take time and money, and the problem facing the neighborhood is immediate and hard to quantify.

Now that the Coopers' interest in selling the house overlaps with our interest in selling it to a buyer more compatible with the atmosphere of the neighborhood, we'd be moved to seek solutions to a problem that has become mutual. We might, for instance, explore the possibility of creating a neighborhood loan fund. After all, if our response would otherwise be a legal one, we'd have to be shelling out money to attorneys. Wouldn't it be better to apply those financial resources directly to the problem rather than to the process for resolving the problem? If a loan fund seems extreme, we might all consult

> *"It is sometimes only when our differences place us directly at odds with our fellows that we bother making the effort to find where our similarities lie."*

our own connections to help Rochelle find a new job. The woman who lives across the street from us is a financial consultant. She might be able to help the neighbors come up with a plan that decreases their expenses to a level that would allow them to continue making mortgage payments. Though neither my husband nor I have legal expertise in foreclosure or bankruptcy, we know attorneys who do and who might be willing to provide the Coopers with a free consultation.

The story of the Coopers' possible foreclosure illustrates two major conflict resolution principles. The first is that conflict is not necessarily a bad thing. It is sometimes only when our differences place us directly at odds with our fellows that we bother making the effort to find where our similarities lie. Which takes us to the second major conflict resolution principle highlighted by the Cooper-neighborhood dilemma. If we focus our efforts on being *right* about the problem—that the zoning laws prohibit the sale of the Cooper house to a fraternity—we are less likely to *solve* it through an exploration of mutual interests.

In this case, N is not only for Neighbor, but also for the necessary conflicts that lead us to unite in action to solve problems at the neighborhood, community, state, national, and international levels.

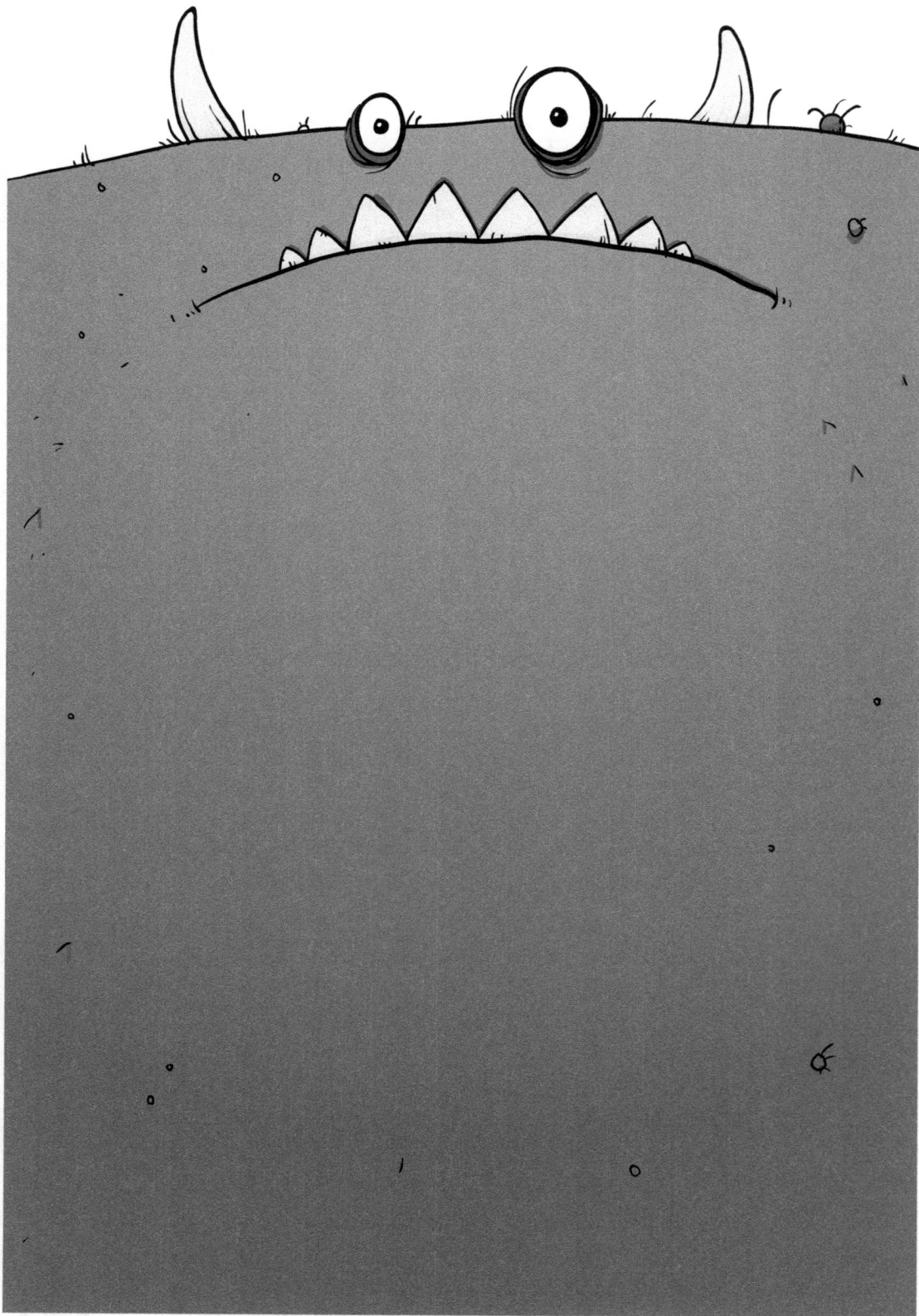

O

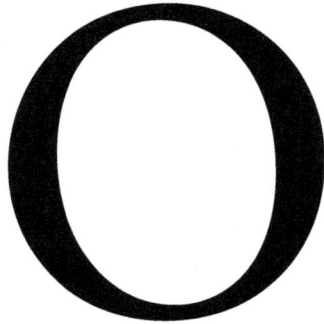

O is for Outlaw

Nearly every condominium complex harbors an outlaw—man, woman, or child—who refuses to follow the rules. It could be the young couple blasting the woofers off their stereo at three a.m., the elderly woman who doesn't clean up after her dog, or the raucous family playing Marco Polo in the community pool after midnight.

Offended and outraged, other homeowners make demands on their board of directors who contact an often-unresponsive management company for help. Volunteer board members issue warnings to no avail. Eventually someone reads the rules governing relationships among the homeowners—the Covenants, Conditions and Restrictions (CC&Rs)—and learns that the board has enforceable legal duties and the homeowners have enforceable legal rights.

Many of these disputes make their way to the Dispute Resolution Center of the Los Angeles County Bar Association in West Hollywood, and some of them make their way to me.

Welcome to community mediation. We're well-trained and we're free, but can we deliver justice?

Condominium owners John and Betty Jones were being driven to distraction by their neighbors who often arrived home to their upstairs apartment at two a.m. only to commence what seemed—to John and Betty—like a Pekinese rodeo. Though John and Betty had asked the officers of their homeowners' association to enforce the rules requiring residents to be quiet after ten p.m., the association had taken no action. Eventually, this dispute made its way my office in the West Hollywood Dispute Resolution Center, located in the spare room of a local Methodist church.

John had practically memorized the CC&Rs governing the board's duties and the homeowner's rights. Betty repeatedly broke into tears as she described sleepless nights spent on the living room couch, where the upstairs neighbor's early-morning antics were the least disturbing. The volunteer board member was sympathetic, but at a loss for solutions. She'd contacted management and sent warnings to the miscreants, to no avail.

"Only punitive measures would do at this point," said John. The CC&Rs called for sanctions to be imposed on rule-breakers, but lacked a means of implementation and enforcement. The homeowners' association representative indicated that she not only had the board's authority to settle the matter, but to impose any necessary and reasonable rules to flesh out the CC&Rs inadequate policies.

John and Betty had been treated badly by their neighbors and unfairly by their homeowners' association. But is unfair treatment also unjust?

In a democratic society, justice is a matter of agreement—usually achieved by voting for representatives who promise to make the laws we want, or by directly voting for or against said laws. At least one legal scholar has suggested that this type of "democratic" justice will not produce fairness unless the people voting on society's rules do so without knowing what their place in that social order will be—top, bottom, or middle. If we didn't know what place we'd have in a proposed new economic or social order, we would not tolerate inequalities unless they benefited those who were the least well off.

Back at the West Hollywood Dispute Resolution Center, John was insisting that the homeowner board impose monetary sanctions against his outlaw neighbors. Not only sanctions, he insisted, but penalties that could be backed up by liens against their property.

"What about notice?" I asked. "And a hearing? There's nothing in the rules about the procedure for imposing sanctions."

"Give them only twenty-four hours notice!" shouted John. "If they don't comply, impose a five hundred dollar sanction to be made a lien against their property. And another five hundred for every day they continue to violate the noise restrictions in the CC&Rs."

I wondered aloud whether Mr. and Mrs. Jones understood that their scofflaw neighbors could use those rules against them.

> *"The opposite of outlaw is order— an order to which all parties would willingly submit for their own personal benefit and that of their community as well."*

"Oh." Silence.

"What set of rules do you think would be fair?" I asked.

Two hours later, we had achieved what my constitutional law professor would have called procedural due process—a set of rules that gave everyone notice and an opportunity to be heard before any sanction could be imposed upon them. These are the rules that flowed from the Joneses naturally, once they realized that the private law they were creating would apply not only to outlaws, but to law-abiding citizens as well.

Whether the principle of fairness is hard-wired into us or culturally controlled, we seem to naturally drive the law toward justice whenever we realize that the next ox to be gored may be our own. In the *ABCs of Conflict Resolution* the opposite of outlaw is order—an order to which all parties would willingly submit for their own personal benefit and that of their community as well.

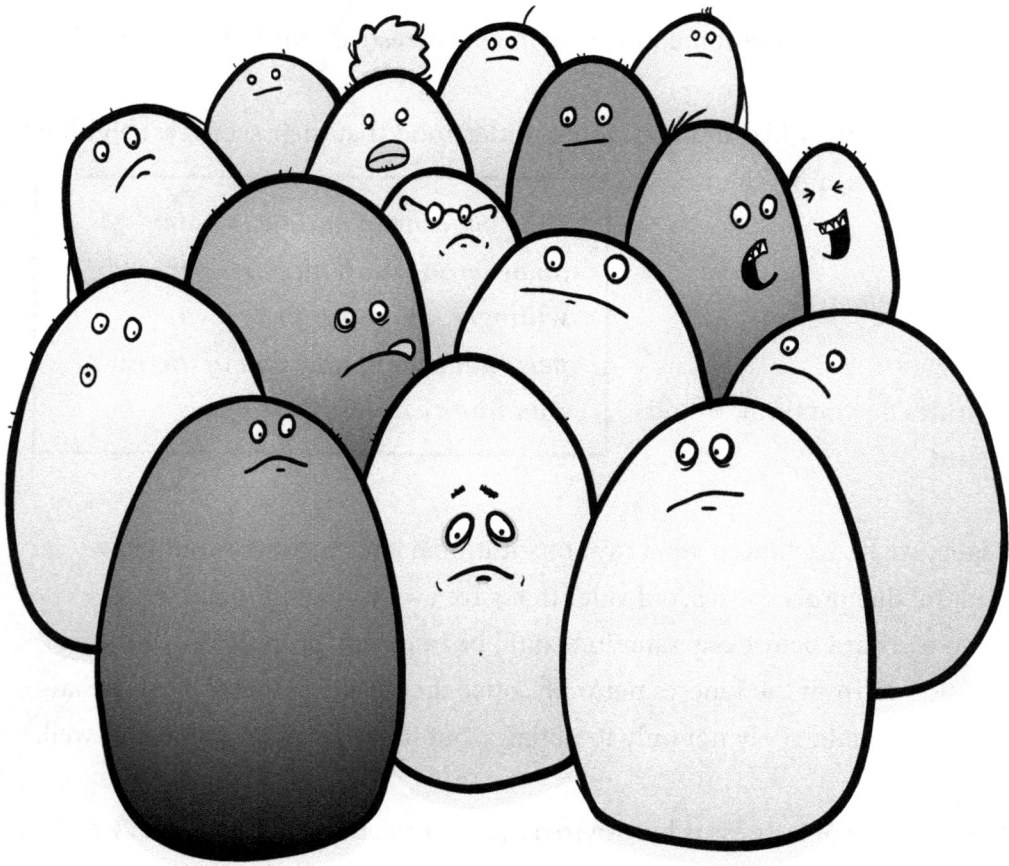

P

P is for Paranoid

These people are paranoid. They believe someone, everyone, is out to get them. They also believe most conspiracy theories ever devised by the mind of man. September eleventh was a hoax devised by the Bush administration as an excuse to attack Iraq. Americans never landed on, let alone set foot upon, the moon. NASA and other federal authorities filmed the antics of actors on a lunar sound stage in Hollywood. Barack Obama is the bastard son of Malcolm X. John F. Kennedy was killed by the mob, by Cubans, by the FBI, by Lyndon Johnson, by the CIA, by the Secret Service, and of course, by the Israelis at whose door so many worldwide domination conspiracy theories are laid.

Psychologists tell us that we are not only "meaning-making" beings, but that we are all born conspiracy theorists. Viewing a field of nonsensical, unrelated data, we naturally begin to connect the dots, to organize what we hear and see into a coherent, and often compelling, narrative. And so it is with our disputes with others—particularly when conflict avoidance, or suits at law, cut off relations with our perceived opponents. Once the channels of communication have been severed, we have no means of reality-testing our most outrageous fantasies. As a result, we weave wild and improbable tales about "what really happened" based on predispositions, scattered conversations, faulty memories, and scraps of documentation.

As a mediator, I hear conspiracy theories on a weekly basis. They are not as glamorous or insidious as the conspiracy theories discussed above, but they are just as ill conceived. Because we often stop talking to the people with whom we are in conflict, it's easy—even natural—to tell ourselves tall tales about people who have become our enemies. That's what Martin, a representative of the Custom Mobile Home Company, did in response to the "lemon-law" action that I mediated one wet, winter afternoon. The plaintiffs, Kirk Townsend and John Finn, purchased a new Custom Mobile Home, drove it a few hundred miles, and had it serviced on four separate occasions for the same set of malfunctions. They hired an attorney and sued Custom Mobile Home. They wanted to return the RV to the manufacturer and get their money back, which they would be entitled to do if the vehicle was legally a "lemon."

Martin couldn't directly check out the plaintiffs' claims, so he made up his own story, one based on stereotypes flowing from the fact that Kirk and John were gay. During a separate meeting with Martin and his attorney, both were absolutely convinced that Kirk and John had acted on a whim and then looked for any excuse they could find to rid themselves of the RV. Once stereotyped, Kirk and John's motivation to bring a lemon law suit seemed obvious to Martin. The plaintiffs had buyer's regret, as any gay men *would*—they had purchased a vehicle so at odds with Martin's stereotype for homosexuals.

When I met separately with Kirk and John in a conference room down the hall, the buyers' remorse story quickly fell to pieces. Kirk was a Vietnam veteran and a lifelong motor home enthusiast. An engineer by profession, he was an auto mechanic by avocation. He and John had been domestic partners for twenty-five years. John sported a crewcut and wore a plaid flannel shirt. Everything about these two men in their late fifties challenged the stereotypes perpetrated by television programs such as *Will and Grace*.

In an effort to undermine Martin's unsupported, but unshakeable theory of his defense, I asked the parties to meet in what mediators call a "joint session"—meaning simply that everyone sits in the same room to discuss the dispute. Before that meeting, I coached Kirk and John to make their narrative short and non-rancorous. I also recommended to Martin that he take a "customer satisfaction/we want to hear your story" approach.

It was not, however, my coaching that settled the lawsuit that day.

As the men shook hands and defense counsel slid into his chair at the conference table, he confirmed something I'd mentioned to him before the meeting. "You're a veteran?" he asked Kirk.

"Army," Kirk replied. "I was in Saigon just before the Tet Offensive."

"Really?" defense counsel asked, leaning forward with genuine interest. "I was in Saigon then, too. Do you remember the X Bar at the end of Y Street?"

For the more cynically minded, this is called a *granfalloon,* a term coined by Kurt Vonnegut in his best-selling science fiction novel, *Cat's Cradle.* It is defined as a group of people who outwardly choose or claim to have a shared identity or purpose, but whose mutual association is actually meaningless. The most common *granfalloons* are associations and societies based on a shared, but ultimately fabricated premise. As examples, Vonnegut cites in "the Communist Party, the Daughters of the American Revolution, the General Electric Company, the International Order of Odd Fellows, and any nation, anytime, anywhere."

For the less cynical, this is simply a quick way in which we establish friendly connections with strangers. It is a way to make patterns of unrelated, and perhaps meaningless, detail signal "home" rather than "danger." In this case, the *granfalloon* of service in Saigon before the Tet Offensive had the effect of breaking down the gay stereotypes on which the defense buyer's-remorse theory rested. As the prejudices crumbled, so did suspicions of a bad-faith claim. When the parties once again repaired to their separate corners, the offers and counter-offers came quickly, and without great resistance.

The mental shortcuts we reflexively use to make snap decisions about strangers' trustworthiness—assumptions often resting on very little evidence—can and usually do prevent us from finding our bargaining partners' true preferences, motivations, priorities, and desires. In the absence of that information, all we have to negotiate with is money—a poor substitute for whatever it is the parties are really seeking to accomplish. Here, Martin connected the unrelated dots of "gay men," "motor home," and "lemon law claim" and drew the conclusion that his company was being cheated and abused. When he talked to Kirk, the dots of "soldier," "mechanic," and "engineer" made better sense when connected to "defective motor home" than to "buyers' remorse."

As the two men fell into easy conversation about the problems Kirk had with the RV and had been unable to fix, Martin finally began hearing the problem. Just as Martin stopped demonizing Kirk and John, Kirk stopped thinking of Martin as a corrupt

> *"P is for Paranoid because the conspiracies we tend to see are at the source of so many disputes that arise among us."*

and greedy representative of a soulless corporation. The men stopped trying to be *right* and were instead focused on the problem at hand—could the vehicle be fixed? The discussion was lively, and I simply watched and listened, knowing that Kirk and Martin, with their lawyers' advice and assistance, would reach an agreement that did not leave the bitter taste of compromise and injustice in their mouths.

In the *Conflict Resolution ABC's*, P is for Paranoid because the conspiracies we tend to see are at the source of so many disputes that arise among us. When we recognize our tendency to find patterns in unrelated events, we are far more likely to ask the questions that will reveal the benign or even charitable motives of our fellows. When we all begin to behave in this manner, P will stand less for paranoid and more for Peace.

Q

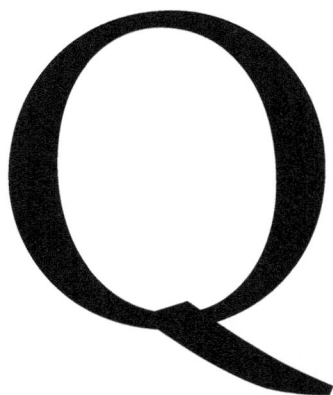

Q is for Questioner

Questions. That's what mediators do for a living. They ask people questions in an effort to find the true source of the parties' conflict and the mutual interests that might resolve their dispute. The tools of the mediation trade are not the coercive, contentious tactics used by litigators, but the exploratory, open-ended questions asked by every journalist and investigator since God asked Adam who gave him the fruit from the tree of knowledge. Only after asking who, what, where, when, why, and how, do we reach the final question—whether we deserve to inhabit the Garden of Eden.

The small, stuffy conference room in a tall Century City office building was nowhere near the Garden of Eden on the last Friday of 2009. I'd spent nearly ten hours in that conference room helping two lawyers and their angry clients reach an agreement to settle a lawsuit about the shipment of allegedly substandard goods. The room was redolent of old pizza, burnt coffee, and the pipe smoke that clung to Mr. Metcalf's tweed sports coat. Metcalf, the plaintiff and purchaser, manages a major retail chain. He is seeking recompense from the defendants, the manufacturer of the porcelain figurines at issue and the shipping company that brought them to Los Angeles from Taiwan. The manufacturer's representative, Mr. Wong, a businessman in Los Angeles, doesn't have a lot of money, but he did have enough to settle this case.

It's late. Everyone has party plans, but Mr. Wong is backsliding. Even his attorney cannot convince him to pay as much money to the purchaser as he'd been willing to pay just two hours earlier. We are failing to persuade, and we are out of arguments. The settlement proposal now on the table makes economic sense. It's good for business. Trial is approaching. The chances are less than even. Everyone is taking a loss. If it's wrong or unfair, it's no worse than a random car wreck—one of life's bad accidents, best left in the past. Trial is worse than uncertain; it portends a bad—and avoidable—result.

Still. The money is coming off the table. I am missing something.

"I'm missing something," I say.

Mr. Wong looks at me with interest for the first time in hours.

"What are you missing?" he asks.

"I don't know. I only know you want to settle the case, but I'm not helping you do that right now. Can you tell me what I can do differently or better?"

Mr. Wong returns to an old theme—a horse I'd assumed we'd beaten to death several hours ago—that his codefendant, the shipping company, should be contributing more, which it has resolutely refused to do.

Finally, it occurs to me that Mr. Lee does not believe I am negotiating hard enough for him.

"Do you think I'm not negotiating hard enough with your codefendant?"

He lights up. "Yes."

"OK. If you give me a counter, I'll work harder to get more money from the shipping company," I say, realizing that I haven't been pressing the codefendant as hard as I could. "Don't press!" I hear my mediation mentors saying in the back of my head. "Explore. Ask questions."

Back in the room in which the plaintiff and his attorney are impatiently waiting, I say, "We're at an impasse because Mr. Wong insists his codefendant knew the facts that the documentation suggests did not occur."

The plaintiff nods vigorously. "That's true," he says, offering a detailed and credible account that contradicts the written record, but dovetails with Mr. Wong's account. Hour Six. Case Settled. And all it took was another small, but significant, contribution by the codefendant.

There is magic in asking people in conflict questions—questions that Kellogg School of Management professor, Leigh Thompson, calls "diagnostic." A diagnostic question, she tells us, is one that reveals our bargaining partner's preferences. She also tells us that only seven percent of all negotiators seek information about party preferences, even when it would be dramatically helpful for them to do so.

> *"A diagnostic question, she tells us, is one that reveals our bargaining partner's preferences."*

What was Mr. Wong's preference? That I press his codefendant to put more money on the table. Did Mr. Wong need more money? No, but his preference that I exert greater effort on his behalf was so strong that my failure to do so caused him to retaliate against me by giving me less authority in Hour Five than he'd given me in Hour Four. I genuinely believed I'd done the best I could, but I was wrong. By how much? Not much. There was more value to be gained, and I had given up. Mr. Wong knew it intuitively, because negotiation is the resolution of a problem by way of communication, and communication is not simply the language of words, but also of feelings, hunches, and intuition.

What took me so long? That constant enemy of clear communication—fear. I didn't want to acknowledge that I wasn't "getting it," even to myself. When I did understand that I wasn't getting it, however, I promptly admitted to it, because of something I'd learned as a mediator.

When you acknowledge vulnerability and imperfection, you open the channel for truth to enter the room. Mr. Wong could finally be frank and open with me, because I'd been transparent with him, and that made the difference between resolving the dispute and not making a deal.

Q is for Questioner because resolution belongs to the curious, the open-minded, and the brave.

R

R is for Romeo

Romeo—the most impulsive and misguided romantic hero in the history of Western literature—has much to teach us about the way conflict unfolds, how we resolve disputes in the absence of a strong, central legal authority, what family means, and what dangers lurk when inexperienced peacemakers try to negotiate peace in "honor cultures."

Because most of the English-speaking world honors the rule of law more than the strong man's dictate, we often recoil from the type of tribal violence that expresses itself in cultures like the one in which the tragic tale of Romeo and Juliet unfolds. As social science popularizer, Malcolm Gladwell, explains in his book *Outliers*, people descended from herding cultures such as those that flourished in the Mediterranean—where Shakespeare sets his scene—whose safety depended upon the creation and maintenance of public reputations for violence. As Gladwell explains,

A herdsman is off by himself [and] is under constant threat of ruin through the loss of his animals. So he has to be aggressive: he has to make it clear through his words and deeds that he is not weak. He has to be willing to fight in response to even the slightest challenge to this reputation—and that's what a "culture of honor" means. It's a world where a man's reputation is at the center of his livelihood and self-worth.

Members of honor cultures meet outsiders with a suspicion so finely tuned that violent retaliation follows slights that rule-of-law cultures can safely ignore. You're rude to my sister. I call you a boor. You brandish a knife. I grab my gun. You lunge. I shoot. You lie in the street, blood pooling around your head, and I flee for my life. Your brothers watch you die. They break into my father's house and kill my uncle. Now we have a family feud, a gang war or tribal border skirmish that will continue in escalating cycles of violence into generations not yet born.

Which brings us back to Romeo, and his American counterpart, Tony, in the 1960s musical *West Side Story*. In both plays, much is made of the warring families' contempt for the law. In Romeo and Juliet, the law is the Prince who chronically complains about his subjects' predictable refusal to follow his edicts. In *West Side Story*, the law is personified by the hapless Officer Krupke, a racist clown who is as disrespected by the Sharks as he is by the Jets. In fact, the gangs' contempt for Krupke is the only point on which they agree.

In both plays, a cycle of escalating violence is set into motion by a casual insult. In Romeo and Juliet, a member of the Capulet family makes a rude hand gesture in the direction of a group of Montagues. Tony and Maria's star-crossed fate begins with an exchange of insults choreographed by Jerome Kern, set to music by Leonard Bernstein, and put into words by Stephen Sondheim. In both cases, the stage is set for violence and for boundary-crossing love.

At the Capulet ball and at the high school dance, Romeo meets Juliet and Tony meets Maria. Juliet's family, the Capulets, and Maria's people, the Puerto Ricans, are at war with their beloveds' kin. Romeo is a Montague to Juliet's Capulet, and Tony is an American to Maria's Puerto Rican family. Tony is a Jet, and Maria's relatives are

Sharks. But love—crazy, sudden, irrational, passionate, teenage love—trumps family and gang loyalty and leaves both couples to ponder the meaning of their group identity as it grinds against the grain of forbidden love. "When love comes so strong," Maria sings, "there is no right or wrong." This is a transcendent love. Freed from the bonds of blood loyalty and the bitter hatred of ancient feuds, all four lovers respond as if newborn. This new loyalty, grounded in emotion rather than history, is so momentous that each experiences a crisis of identity. Because allegiance to historical ties is wholly incompatible with love for one's enemy, and because teenage love is stronger than storied animosity, it is the conflict that must vanish and the self that must be transformed.

"What *is* Montague?" Juliet asks of Romeo's last name from her legendary balcony. Her answer to the question is nothing short of revolutionary.

"'Tis but thy name that is my enemy," Juliet dares to think. And Romeo, she concludes, is a "self" with an identity separate from his family ties. Therefore, Romeo need not be her enemy and can be her love. In her famous soliloquy, Juliet separates each physical part of Romeo from the name that would prohibit their union. Romeo's name—his *family*—"is not hand nor foot, nor arm, nor face, nor any other part belonging to a man." Not knowing Romeo lurks in the garden below, Juliet beseeches him to "doff thy name and for that name, which is no part of thee, take all myself."

Let's pause for a moment here to fully take in the meaning of this moment in the history of human relations. In fewer than two dozen lines, Juliet has moved from asking what family means, to deciding it means nothing, to offering her hand in marriage to her family's most hated enemy.

What is in a name? In an honor culture, it is *everything*—safety, loyalty, honor, purpose, self. Romeo, equally liberated and equally daft, is hiding in the bushes as Juliet declares her new allegiance to him. He, too, is willing to throw off his old sense of identity and be someone new. "Call me but love," he exclaims, "and I'll be new baptized. Henceforth I never will be Romeo."

The year is 1591. America has not yet been discovered. Yet here is Shakespeare suggesting what a bunch of scruffy hippies in San Francisco's Golden Gate Park would be singing about nearly four hundred years later. "All you need is love." It is in this moment—echoed by Tony and Maria's metaphoric marriage in the dress shop—that the new generation transcends their parents', and their parents' parents' conflicts, opening possibilities for themselves and their families that never before existed.

This is what mediators and peacemakers are talking about when they speak of conflict transcendence and transformation. As mediator, lawyer, educator, and author, Dr. Kenneth Cloke, observes in his book, *The Crossroads of Conflict*:

> *Every conflict presents the parties... with a... choice. They can cling to safe territory, keep the conversation focused on relatively superficial issues, and avoid mentioning deeper topics, remaining locked in impasse and placing their lives on hold. Or they can take a risk, adopt a more open, honest, empathic approach and initiate a deeper, more dangerous, heartfelt conversation that could change their lives and result in transformation and transcendence. Which path they take will depend partly on their willingness to engage each other in heartfelt communications.*

By virtue of their "heartfelt communications," all four lovers are forever altered. The way they experience their previously narrow world, and the certainty they feel in their new place in it, can never be the same. As Cloke explains:

> *Transcendence occurs when people gain insight into the attitudes, intentions, and perceptions that sustained their conflict, improve their ability to learn from it, work collaboratively to prevent its reoccurrence, and evolve to higher levels of conflict and resolution.*

Tragically, the world does not transform itself, nor transcend its ancient grievances just because a couple of teenagers fall in love. The teens are in danger. Grave danger. Tony naïvely believes he can broker a fair fight between the Sharks and the Jets, assuring his mentor, Doc, proprietor of the local soda fountain, "From here on in, everything's gonna be all right."

Doc: What have you been takin' tonight?

Tony: A trip to the moon. And I'll tell ya a secret, Doc. It ain't a man that's up there. It's a girl.

Doc: So that's why you made it a fair fight.

Tony: I'm gonna see her tomorrow, and I can't wait.

Doc: Things aren't tough enough?

Tony: Doc, I'm in love.

Doc: And you're not frightened?

Tony: Should I be?

Doc: No, I'm frightened enough for the both of you.

Doc knows what Tony does not. If Tony, transformed, returns to the streets to seek a negotiated peace, the culture will expel him. To members of honor cultures, any attempt to negotiate the peaceful resolution of historic wounds and ancient grudges puts the entire family, gang, or tribe at risk. To talk with the other side in a non-belligerent manner, and to listen in the same way to one's enemy puts the negotiator in a vulnerable position. That vulnerability does not affect only the negotiator, particularly where he is also a community leader. It puts the entire tribe at risk of victimization. In the absence of a strong, central, legal authority to police and punish those who would prey on the weak, a carefully cultivated fear of immediate, disproportionate, and violent retaliation serves as the only protection against harm.

You can see this tragedy coming long before Romeo, returning to the field of conflict, turns his back on the call to arms by Juliet's cousin, Tybalt. When Romeo arrives in the town square, the young men of the Montague and Capulet tribes have been trading insults. Tybalt, enraged by the Montagues' trespass upon his uncle's property the night before—the night of the ball at which Romeo and Juliet met and pledged their love—is demanding that Romeo appear for a fight. The Montagues have been disrespected. They need to—are expected to—retaliate.

Romeo arrives and refuses the challenge. If Romeo will not respond, another must. Mercutio, Romeo's cousin, obeying the dictates of all honor cultures everywhere, draws his sword and hisses at his cousin Romeo, "O calm, dishonorable, vile submission!" Romeo is shaming his family by refusing to defend its honor.

Though unschooled in the resolution of conflict, Romeo attempts in vain to avert the pending fight by using a few contentious dispute resolution tactics. He is ingratiating with Mercutio, imploring him with an endearment to put down his sword—"gentle Mercutio, put thy rapier up." When Tybalt and Mercutio begin to fight, Romeo tries out shame. "Gentlemen!" he shouts as they thrust and parry. "For shame, forbear this outrage!" Panicking, Romeo attempts an appeal to a higher authority. "Tybalt, Mercutio," he exhorts, "the Prince expressly hath forbidden bandying in Verona's streets. Hold, Tybalt! Good Mercutio." Then Romeo makes the fatal error. He resorts to physical force, standing in front of Mercutio and attempting to push Tybalt back, giving Tybalt the opportunity to stab Mercutio under Romeo's arm.

"Why the devil came you between us?" Mercutio demands. "I was hurt under your arm." As he dies on the street, betrayed by his kinsman, fatally wounded in a fight not his own, Mercutio rages, "A plague o' both your houses!"

So much for peace-making. Romeo awakens from his lover's haze. His "reputation stain'd with Tybalt's slander," he does what men have been doing since Adam ate the apple. He blames Juliet. She has "soften[ed] his valour's steel," poor boy. Tybalt returns and Romeo retaliates as his honor culture demands, leaving Tybalt, Juliet's *brother*, dead in the street.

Following the plot laid down hundreds of years before, in *West Side Story* Tony kills Maria's brother in the rumble Tony naïvely believed would be fought fair and only with fists. Anita breaks the news to Maria, not knowing that Tony, *her* lover's murderer, is Maria's lover. When she learns the truth, she sings bitterly,

116

A boy like that who'd kill your brother,
Forget that boy and find another,
One of your own kind-
Stick to your own kind!

A boy like that will give you sorrow-
You'll meet another boy tomorrow!
One of your own kind,
Stick to your own kind!

Maria's ardor prevails, and Anita agrees to arrange a meeting between her and Tony. Meanwhile, back in Verona, Friar Tuck is giving Juliet a potion that mimics death, but only puts her to sleep. The Friar hopes the two families will be startled into the recognition that their feud is killing those whom they most cherish. He tries to warn Romeo, but his letter is intercepted. Anita tries to contact Tony, but his gang taunts and nearly rapes her. Enraged, Anita hisses, "I'll give you a message for your American buddy! Tell the murderer Maria's never going to meet him! Tell him Chino found out and shot her!"

> *"Only when all families suffer a simultaneous, catastrophic loss—when their injuries can be blamed on nothing and no one other than the senseless feud—do they finally break through to the metaphysical truth that Romeo and Juliet so recently learned in the garden."*

Tony and Romeo, believing their beloveds to be dead, court their own deaths—Romeo by plunging Juliet's dagger into his heart, and Tony by calling out to Chino, "Come on: get me too!" Chino does get him, and Tony dies in Maria's arms.

Only when all families suffer a simultaneous, catastrophic loss—when their injuries can be blamed on nothing and no one other than the senseless feud—do they finally break through to the metaphysical truth that Romeo and Juliet so recently learned in the garden. What is in a name? What is Montague and what is Capulet? What is Puerto Rican and what is American?

The Prince arrives, asking, "Where be these enemies? Capulet! Montague! See what a scourge is laid upon your hate that finds means to kill your joys with love and I for winking at your discords too have lost a brace of kinsmen. All are punish'd."

And the story of New York's West Side? When Tony dies, Maria takes Chino's gun and asks,

> *How do you fire this gun, Chino? Just by pulling this little trigger? How many bullets are left, Chino? Enough for you? And you? All of you? WE ALL KILLED HIM, and my brother, and Riff. I, too. I CAN KILL NOW, BECAUSE I HATE NOW. How many can I kill, Chino? How many—and still have one bullet left for me?*

Maria throws the gun from her. One of Tony's gang members takes her shawl and puts it over her head, as if she were the Virgin Mary mourning the death of her son. The stage directions take special care to tell us that the "adults" who tolerate prejudice and hate are "bowed, alone, useless" as the Sharks and the Jets together leave the stage.

No one is without sin, and all are punished.

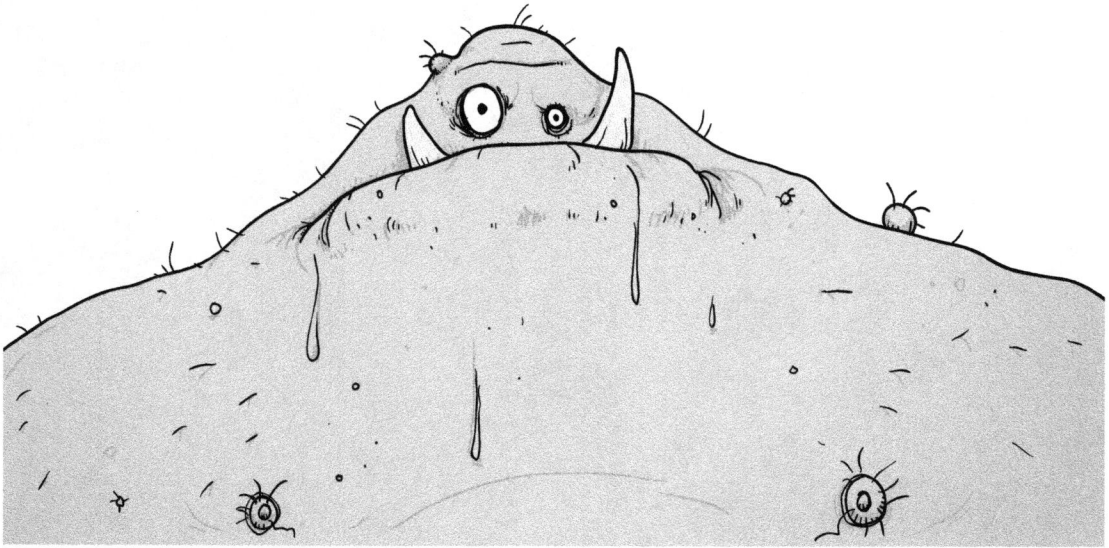

S

S is for Shakedown Artist

Some people are skilled in the art of the shakedown. They ask for your money or your life. They point a gun at your head while taking the watch off your arm. They don't ask, they coerce. They don't bargain, they impose their will by threatening to expose your misdeeds. They are blackmailers and extortionists, gangsters and thieves.

But wait a minute. Those aren't shakedown artists, are they? They look like... lawyers!

Many people who are sued in a court of law feel as if they're being extorted. Litigation, you'll recall, is a contentious dispute-resolution tactic. Other tactics include ingratiation (seeking sympathy for your plight), gamesmanship (shunning), threats (see you in court), arguments (I deserve X, and you must give it to me because the law requires it), shaming (a common tactic of street demonstrators and union boycotters), and coercive commitments (if you don't answer this lawsuit, a judgment will be issued against you).

When a process server arrives at your door with a summons and complaint, he is delivering a threat. In California, that threat appears on a document called a summons, which predicts the entry of judgment against you if you do not file the right papers in the right place by the right time. Respond with the right legal form or you may be stripped of all your worldly goods.

You generally do not pick up the telephone after you've suffered the shock of being sued. You're more likely to retaliate by hiring your own lawyer and filing a claim of your own. The fight has only just begun, and the contentious tactic that initiated this cursed dispute will escalate over time. Lawyers will be hired to press your version of the facts and argue your interpretation of the law. They will do so by filing motions, asking the court to dismiss the case before trial. Your opponent will make burdensome requests for discovery requiring you to answer questions in writing under oath, to appear before a court reporter in a lawyer's office to answer questions orally under penalty of perjury, and to produce every document in your files that has even a tangential relationship to the issues raised by the lawsuit.

Your lawyers have instructed you not to talk to your opponent, because anything you say can and will be used against you. Unable to clarify misunderstandings or come to a shared understanding about the expensive legal maneuvering in which your expensive attorneys are engaged, you will naturally interpret every move by your adversary in the worst possible light. You are now in a state that social psychologists call "autistic hostility."

Autism is a state of being, cut off from the outside world. It is self-referential and rarely, if ever, tested against the perceived reality of others. If we break off a relationship with someone at a time when our feelings toward that person are hostile, we tend to interpret everything that person does as furthering—and often exaggerating and escalating—the hostility between us. Professor Morton Deutsch at Columbia University describes this state in relationship to the taste of coffee.

"I never drink coffee," he writes. "I avoid any taste of coffee, like coffee ice cream. I may be mistaken about coffee. Maybe I would like it if I experienced it, if I had contact with coffee. If I had communicated, so to speak. If I allowed coffee to communicate with me, it would change my attitude. That's one thing that happens sometimes in conflict. You maintain your hostility autistically, within yourself, without any necessary reactor."

In the absence of a "necessary reactor," our cognitive biases will generally override any possibility that our adversary is acting out of fear, or loss, or some other benign state of being. The fundamental attribution error described in the chapter "I is for Idiot" will cause us to ascribe intentionality to the burden, expense, and stress that the mere existence of the lawsuit causes us. Confirmation bias—the tendency to search for, interpret, or remember information in a way that confirms our preconceptions—will paint every activity in which our opponent is engaged as one emphasizing his contentious, disrespectful, even evil, nature and intent. And reactive devaluation—the tendency to diminish the attractiveness or value of any proposal that comes from someone we perceive as an adversary—will make it difficult or impossible to negotiate a resolution to the lawsuit.

> "The Shakedown Artist, it turns out, feels as justified in his position as does the defendant he sued."

The solution?

Though there are circumstances in which lawsuits must be filed to resolve a dispute that the parties need the force of law to settle, litigation should be a last—not an initial —dispute resolution strategy. If the parties are unable to resolve a particularly difficult conflict themselves, they should consider seeking the help of a third party, such as a mediator to help them overcome the cognitive biases that might otherwise prevent them from reaching a cost-effective and relationship-saving solution. The Shakedown Artist, it turns out, feels as justified in his position as does the defendant he sued. Instead of separating these parties, instructing them not to speak to one another, and watching the inevitable demonization and confirmation bias processes, we could sit them down together in a room and ask them a few diagnostic questions. Those questions would include:

- What was your relationship like before it became troubled?
- What happened?
- How were you injured?
- Do you feel that you were treated unfairly?
- How?
- If you were in your opponent's shoes, how do you think you'd respond to this event?
- Have you talked to your opponent about this event and its consequences?
- Would you be willing to hear his or her side of the story?
- Can you think of any way that your concerns might be satisfied at the same time that your opponent's needs or desires are supported?
- In the best of all possible worlds, what would your relationship with your opponent be after you've resolved the dispute that brought you to your lawyer?
- Do you believe you played any part whatsoever in either the event giving rise to the dispute, or the way in which the dispute was handled by either party?

These are just a few of the dozens of questions that might be posed to warring parties in an effort to seek a resolution that requires neither to be "right" and neither to be "wrong." While having a conversation about the dispute, remember your own cognitive biases—your tendency to listen only for the facts that support your position and to discard anything that does not; your tendency to ascribe any injury causing event to your opponent's intention and to minimize your contribution by ascribing it to circumstance; your tendency to demonize your opponent to minimize the possibility that you might sympathize with him or her, thereby decreasing the strength of your claims to redress.

When we take responsibility for our own behavior and listen respectfully to the story of our adversary, we inevitably find a way to resolve a dispute that not only makes us "whole" for our injuries, but which allows us to walk away feeling as if justice has been done.

TU

T is for Them and U is for Us

"We tell ourselves stories in order to live," wrote novelist and essayist, Joan Didion.

The princess is caged in the consulate. The man with the candy will lead the children into the sea. The naked woman on the ledge outside the window is a victim or an exhibitionist, and it would be "interesting" to know which. We tell ourselves that it makes a difference whether she is about to commit a mortal sin or is about to register a political protest or is about to be snatched back to the human condition by the fireman in priest's clothing. We look for the sermon in the suicide, for the social or moral lesson in the murder of five. We interpret what we see, select the most workable of the multiple choices. We live entirely, especially if we are writers, by the imposition of a narrative line upon disparate images, by the "ideas" with which we have learned to freeze the shifting phantasmagoria which is our actual experience.

Joan Didion, The White Album

The small man in the incongruously meticulous three-piece suit and skullcap is sitting behind an enormous desk strewn with files, photos, pleadings, paper clips, and crumpled Styrofoam coffee cups. There is even evidence of yesterday's lunch or maybe last night's late snack—a Fiestaware salad plate smeared with the congealed remains of something unidentifiable. Mr. Segal's face reddens as he stabs his finger repeatedly into a yellow legal pad that carries his firm's embossed name.

"They disrespected my niece," he is repeating, his voice rising with each iteration. "She grew up in Budapest. She knows something about rats."

He is sputtering now, on the verge of losing the professional demeanor I am certain he values. "And that fake Jew—the company's lawyer—his client disrespected her and now they're disrespecting me."

It is nine o'clock on a warm Los Angeles morning, and my business day has just begun. This dispute, on the surface over religious animosity, cloaked in a pest company's failure to rid a house of rats, is somehow tinged with a more profound anger and a deeper fear.

Mr. Segal's Santa Monica law office has one of those unexpectedly magnificent ocean views—the kind that make you feel guilty about an unmerited grace. The counterpoint is unsettling between the ocean view, with swaying palms towering over brightly colored joggers on the Palisade and Mr. Segal's claustrophobic office. Open boxes spill out exhibits from his last trial, and colorful graphic boards lean against the wall. He has already explained the trial victory these graphics helped him achieve—one of numerous injustices rectified by a Los Angeles Superior Court jury.

I used to be in the business of telling these stories myself—pushing the square pegs of my clients' actual experiences, the shifting phantasmagoria, into the round holes of the predetermined American legal conflict narrative I learned in law school. To bring a lawsuit in a court of law, you must allege facts that fit the elements, or requirements, of a cause of action. If you can prove that a service provider failed to provide those services in a reasonably careful manner, and that his failure to do so caused you injury, you are entitled to recover damages—monetary recompense for what you lost.

Fake Jew. The raw emotion of this epithet startles me. I've met with Mr. Segal, counsel for his Eastern European niece, once before. We exchanged pleasantries about the neighborhood in which we both live—one with a large Orthodox and ultra-Orthodox population. He knows that my husband is Jewish and I am not. According to Mr. Segal, "with all due respect," I and my cross-marrying kind will eventually be responsible for the destruction of world Jewry. I'm easy-going on this topic and have not taken offense.

With Mr. Segal's fake Jew accusation, I've hit dispute resolution pay dirt. He is alerting me to the master narrative that I begin to believe is the reason this lawsuit is in the Superior Court in the first place—a narrative of a community splintered and in danger of destruction.

In the *ABCs of Conflict Resolution*, master narratives are filed under the letters "U for Us" and "T for Them." They are the national and religious stories that shape our lives, creating a sense of kinship within the community of us and distinguishing that community from the way that others live. You know the others. The 'others' are them. Peace seekers and dispute resolvers believe that most conflicting us and them narratives can be harmonized, but that resolution depends upon finding common ground.

> *"Peace seekers and dispute resolvers believe that most conflicting Us and Them narratives can be harmonized, but that resolution depends upon finding common ground."*

Mr. Segal is waiting for my response to his accusation—the personal insult flung at opposing counsel, Mr. Klein. I know that Segal is disposed to trust me. I'd accepted his criticism with humor. More importantly, I'd accepted him the way he is—an absolute prerequisite to trust. I was also keeping in mind the advice given to me by mediator and author, Dr. Kenneth Cloke—look for the cry for help lurking beneath every accusation.

"I'm taking a class in Religion and Conflict Resolution," I say casually, partly to bring down the emotional temperature in the room, and partly to get a grip on the role Mr. Segal's Jewish master narrative is playing in the Rat Litigation. "We haven't gotten to Judaism yet. What does the Torah say about peace-making?"

Mr. Segal's mood shifts immediately. The anger drains out of him. Not only is this a comfortable topic, it's something he knows a lot about. He smiles for the first time that morning. "Peace," he says softly. "The Torah requires us to seek peace."

Obviously he's had this discussion before, because he quickly adds, "but only among fellow Jews. We're not required to seek peace with anyone else."

I thank Mr. Segal and ask for the list of his niece's damaged items. I head down the hall to the conference room where Mr. Klein and his client wait for me.

Both snort derisively when I provide them with Mr. Segal's demand. The lawsuit is frivolous, they say. Mr. Klein pulls a sheaf of papers from his briefcase to show me the documents that establish, beyond doubt, that the defense will prevail. I examine the papers. They're ambiguous. That's the thing you learn about lawsuits when you've represented people and businesses for a while—if it takes a lawsuit to resolve the problem, nothing is clear or obvious.

"It's about rats," I say, handing the papers back to Mr. Klein. "Rats make people jumpy. The jurors might respond badly to these pictures."

I pass around some Polaroid shots of dead rats in traps. I can feel the ground shifting under our feet. They are shocked that I am not agreeing with them. They aren't taking it personally, of course, but they are outraged. The suit is extortionate. Mr. Segal might as well be holding a gun to their heads. Why can't I see that?

"I'm not disagreeing with you," I offer. "I just wonder whether trying the case is worth the expense."

I don't want to further inflame the defense, but I wonder what is motivating them to spend so much money fighting this small battle in court. I ask as quietly as I can about the fine that Mr. Segal told me the court has imposed on the defense for failing to provide information to the plaintiff. "Is it worth taking that issue up to the Court of Appeal?" I ask, as Mr. Segal told me the defense was threatening to do.

Mr. Klein turns red. "Mr. Segal," he says, "is a bully. He's like an Israeli soldier in a Palestinian refugee camp."

Another accusation. I ask myself how Palestinian refugees might feel, herded into camps and faced with a show of force—certainly vulnerable; possibly victimized, mistreated, misunderstood, angry, or afraid. The defense will not make a counter-offer. Mr. Klein and his client begin to loudly slam their notebooks, papers, and PDAs into their briefcases—international sign language for 'we're outta here.' Though I don't think further discussion will lead to settlement, I can't help but feel that we still have business to do.

"I like to be helpful," I say to Mr. Klein and his client as they prepare to leave. "I'm sorry I was unable to help you resolve the litigation. I can, if you would like, try to help the parties proceed without further unnecessary acrimony."

"What is this?" Mr. Klein snaps. "Some kind of new-age trick?"

"No," I say, "just a question. If you think you might be able to get to trial more quickly and at less expense in a cordial atmosphere, I'm happy to help."

"How could I say no?" asks Mr. Klein, irritably. "It wouldn't be politically correct, would it?"

"I don't think political correctness is the issue," I say. "Some people think it is better to be acrimonious. It makes it unpleasant to litigate. People settle faster and for less."

He pauses. Mr. Klein's client must be concerned by the sanction imposed by the court, and by the size of his attorney's fees. Mr. Klein must be concerned about his own role in this mess. I don't want to leave him defenseless—like a Palestinian in an Israeli refugee camp.

"I've done it myself," I say. "It's a tactical, not a moral, issue. It's a choice."

Mr. Klein and his client turn to one another for a quick, whispered conference.

"OK," they say, both nodding.

"You won't get anywhere," warns Mr. Klein, "but go ahead and try."
Back in Mr. Segal's office, my news is met with a flat, "You want me to apologize?"

I shrug and smile ruefully.

"There's nothing to apologize for," he says, beginning to redden again.

"Disrespect," he reasserts. "It's not about me. It's about my niece. It's about family." This last assertion is from the Godfather stock of cultural narratives, with a Tony Soprano inflection.

We both know what we are talking about. The last telephone conference had ended with an exchange of insults and profanity.

"Is he going to apologize?"

"I think he'll be willing," I say, believing it.

"That was wrong, telling him to 'go f*** himself.' But the reason I said it remains valid. That wasn't wrong. So, no. No apology."

132

I look out the window. The wind has picked up and morning joggers have given way to noontime strollers. Two college kids are kissing on a park bench. Am I looking to win this mediation by fixing something, anything, for the litigants? I don't think so. I believe I'm trying to do what I think is part of my new job. I turn back to Mr. Segal.

"Mr. Klein is Jewish?" I ask, remembering Mr. Segal's insistence that Jews need only make peace with other Jews. He knows where I'm going. He doesn't need to say yes, but he does. He had, after all, accused his opponent of unraveling the fabric of Jewish history. This isn't just about violating the rules of legal discourse; it's about identity and community.

In the world of Jewish Orthodoxy, the Orthodox are 'us' and the non-Orthodox are 'them'. We believe the world would be more peaceful, that there would be fewer wars, if we could just eliminate them from our sight or expel them from our city. But when they go—the Palestinians Mr. Klein mentioned, for instance—we create new categories of 'them.' In this mediation, there were men of the Jewish faith and culture on both sides of the dispute, and yet much of the heat of the conflict arose from the seemingly conflicting values and differing identities of each man's Jewish community.

"I think you're a moral man, Mr. Segal," I say, pausing to let my observation be confirmed or denied. Mr. Segal is silent.

"Does the Torah call upon you to make peace with a fellow Jew today?" I ask. The small, cluttered office is hot. Phones are ringing down the hallway, and women's voices rise in laughter in the next room.

I do not want to push any harder. I don't know why this dispute is so freighted with religious animosity. It reminds me how easily anger or fear over one problem—a pest company's failure to rid a house of rats—can grab hold of a more profound anger or deeper fear, particularly when we have divided the world up into those who are good and those who are evil, those who we know share our beliefs and those who we firmly believe do not and never will.

I do it myself, I'm afraid, particularly in making the transition from attorney to mediator and arbitrator. Judges and lawyers who are hired by other lawyers to help them settle cases or resolve them privately in arbitration, tend to be older than I am. More important to my own livelihood is the fact that roughly ninety percent of those in commercial or business-to-business mediation and arbitration are men. I've been complaining about them a lot lately. The old white men who dominate the profession. I'd been blaming them for the length of time it was taking me to establish myself as a respected neutral in the legal community. Perhaps it was time for me to stop and take a breath, to focus on the precise task at hand—building my practice—rather than trying to fight the old and tiresome war of the sexes I'd fought on and off since the early 1970s. Perhaps there was something I could learn about the unnecessary animosity between Mr. Orthodox and Mr. Non-Orthodox.

"He's not one of them," I say, finally. "Is he?"

Silence.

"What does the Torah say?"

With that, Mr. Segal gets up, puts on his jacket, and motions toward the door that leads down the hall. "Okay," he says. "I'll do it."

It is one of those moments other people tell you about, but you never expect to experience yourself. It's one of those times when we break through to the metaphysical truth that we are one. All else—the perception that we are separate and independent, that our interests are pitted against one another, that one side of the ship can sink to the ocean floor while the other stays afloat—is a fundamental misunderstanding in the way we know we must treat one another.

The error is corrected in part by complementary storytelling. Peacemakers reframe conflict narratives into stories premised on mutual interest—tales in which the parties hold themselves, and one another, accountable for the creation of mutual harm.

People bring stories of mistrust, betrayal, trauma, and miscommunication to lawyers in the hope that their tales of injustice will be solved in just one way: they will win and the other will lose. Someone in authority—a judge or an arbitrator—will decide that their subjective account of the dispute with another is right and their opponent's account is wrong. To make this contest easier for all, we demonize one another, place the others in a warring camp, and dehumanize them. It's so much easier to compete with someone who is already somehow the enemy, the 'other,' before he even took a swipe at us. His otherness relieves us of the obligation to treat our fellows with compassion. It lets us be hurtful.

In the *ABCs of Conflict Resolution*, we transcend disputes whenever we rise above our all-too-human tendency to take the easy us-or-them road in favor of the road of 'we.' We need only be patient enough—maybe even courageous enough—to look for the more profound, relational truth lying just outside the frame, beyond the open window, or around the corner from the woman standing naked on the ledge. That story is the key to wisdom's door, the secure web that connects us, and the rope thrown out the prison window that can set us free.

V

V is for Victim

Every act of violence requires a victim, and every victim a perpetrator. Even if victim and offender are strangers, in the searing moment when a violent crime is committed, they become inextricably bound in one of the most painful human relationships imaginable.

Lyndy is a victim of violent crime. When we first meet her, she is pregnant with her first child. When we first meet the man who raped her at knifepoint fourteen years earlier, it is her own brother, Tim, to whom we are introduced. Tim is serving the thirteenth of a twenty-year prison sentence for his crime. Lyndy is serving her own kind of sentence, one which can only be commuted by Tim.

Lyndy and Tim's story of violent crime, accountability, forgiveness, and restoration —told in the award-winning documentary, *Beyond Conviction*—reminds us that remedies exist to heal the wounds inflicted by nearly every damaged human relationship.

By anyone's standards, the Pennsylvania criminal justice system has done for Lyndy the job it was supposed to do. Tim was arrested, charged with rape, convicted, and sentenced to twenty years in prison. The punishment meted out to Tim, however, did nothing to help Lyndy recover life as she knew it before that terrifying November night, when Tim came home drunk, flew into a rage, held a knife to Lyndy's throat, forced her upstairs, and repeatedly raped her.

Twelve years after Tim's sentencing, Lyndy found herself close to suicide. If she took her own life, Tim's curse, his terrible prophecy, would come true—that by his hand, Lyndy's life would be ruined. Lyndy perservered, and when she she became pregnant two years later, she sought out the services of Pennsylvania's restorative justice program, a program devoted to doing that which the criminal justice does not, and cannot, do—heal the victim. When asked why she wanted to meet with her brother after so many years, Lyndy explained, "I want to raise my son to be a kind, forgiving, and caring person, and I can't do that if I can't be kind, forgiving, and caring to the one person who has hurt me the most."

Lyndy wants to forgive, but we cannot forgive that which we do not understand. Nor can we forgive someone who is unwilling to take responsibility for the harm he has caused. That would just make us more of a victim—doormats, co-conspirators to our own injury. Lyndy wants—she needs—her brother to acknowledge his responsibility for her suffering. She wants to tell him that nothing in their mutually difficult childhood could possibly justify his crime. And like so many victims, she wants to know that the rape was not her fault.

At its best, restorative justice can deliver those benefits to crime victims, benefits no other program has even attempted to provide. Despite the existence of a vigorous victim's rights movement that began in the 1970s, our criminal courts rarely address harm done to crime victims and never attempt to mend the tear in the social fabric that crime creates. Restorative justice is meant to change that.

Though our current understanding of social relations and psychological processes has revolutionized society, politics, and culture, criminal law remains much the same as it was in thirteenth-century Britain and medieval Europe. People accused of crimes are prosecuted in the name of "the people," rather than on behalf of the victim. Other than providing testimony at the time of trial and assistance to law enforcement officials, the victim is more or less ignored. And though some non-violent offenders are sentenced to work-release prisons, where they can earn enough money to pay some restitution to their victims, the criminal justice process rarely addresses the grievous, and often lifelong, harm suffered by victims.

At the same time that victim's rights advocacy groups were forming in the early seventies, the restorative justice movement was born. While the existing criminal justice system has punishment (and sometimes rehabilitation) in mind, its sole purpose is first to determine guilt, and then to prescribe an appropriate punishment. The justice sought is primarily retributive—the criminal must pay for the crime, which is considered an offense against the community rather than against the individual.

> *"Rather than seeking to punish, restorative justice seeks to instill accountability in the offender; to help offender and victim agree upon the type and extent of restitution; to assist the victim in forgiving the offender; and to help the offender return to the community as a law-abiding citizen."*

Restorative justice is relational, rather than punitive. Its practitioners view crime as a profound rupture in the offender's relation to the victim, as well as to the community in which the crime occurred. Rather than seeking to punish, restorative justice seeks to instill accountability in the offender; to help offender and victim agree upon the type and extent of restitution; to assist the victim in forgiving the offender; and to help the offender return to the community as a law-abiding citizen.

The restorative justice process depicted in *Beyond Conviction* is a post-conviction process. Its goals, however, are the same as pre-conviction processes. That's what Lyndy has signed up for in this story—a restorative justice process that she hopes will allow her to move past the trauma of the rape by her brother.

Lyndy and her brother are sitting at a long table in a bare room. The victim-offender mediator sits halfway between them. This mediator, and others, have been preparing for this moment for months. Tim averts his gaze. The atmosphere is as taut as a stretched rubber band. The mediator starts the session by asking Lyndy how she is doing. Lyndy shows Tim a picture of her new infant son. They exchange a few words of small talk. After all, they haven't seen one another since the trial, and they have never before spoken with one another about the rape.

When the awkward exchange of greetings stalls, Lyndy asks the question that has been weighing on her for nearly fifteen years.

"Why me? What did I do?"

That question—what did I do to deserve the harm you caused me—is common among victims. No one ever deserves to be the victim of a crime. Still, we blame the victim, and the victim blames herself.

Why?

Those who blame the victim do so for their own comfort. If the victim is at fault, the rest of us can relax. We haven't done anything that would subject us to such injury. So long as this rape or that murder, this robbery or that burglary, can be blamed on the victim's carelessness, bad judgment, or low moral character, we can continue to deny that violent crime could randomly strike us at any time without warning and without fault.

Victims of violent crime engage in a similar process in an attempt to wrest a sense of control from the chaos of violent crime. Who among us hasn't repetitively recreated the last moments before an accident, thinking and rethinking the infinite number of ways it could have been avoided. "If I'd gotten up ten minutes later, I wouldn't have been in the intersection at the moment the drunk driver ran the red light." "If I'd accepted that second helping of potatoes Mom attempted to ladle on my plate at Sunday diner, the burgler would have been gone by the time I arrived home, and I wouldn't have been shot."

These musings only get us so far. It's hard enough to regain some sense of safety after a violent crime disrupts our peace of mind without blaming ourselves for its occurrence. The temporal explanations ("if I hadn't left the play early . . .") never get to the question they are masking—what did I do to deserve to be treated in this way? The only one who knows the answer is the perpetrator. When he candidly and credibly explains his motives, no matter how misguided or crazy, the victim can finally say, "It wasn't me after all," and the community can finally heave a sigh of relief—"It wasn't our fault either."

The crime remains inexcusable, but it makes sense at last.

Lyndy's question hangs in the air. "Why me?" Tim continues to stare at the table. "I don't know what to say," he finally responds. "Sorry. That's all I've ever wanted to say —sorry."

But "sorry" is not what Lyndy has been waiting fifteen years to hear. Her question is "*Why?*" Tim also hasn't said just what it is he's sorry for. Lyndy persists.

"Why me?" she asks again, tearing up. "What did I do?"

"Oh, gosh," Tim says, still avoiding the question.

"You have to answer my question," she repeats.

Tim doesn't answer, so Lyndy begins. "I trusted you," she says, her voice breaking. "You were supposed to be my brother. You were supposed to protect me, and you did the worst thing anybody… has ever done to me."

Tim sits rigid, clearly ashamed. The decisive moment is nearly upon him—the turning point when he must finally acknowledge to his sister the unspeakable wrong he has done her. When Tim says he's tried as hard as he could to recall the events of the night of the rape, Lyndy asks, "What's stopping you?" Tim is mute. Lyndy presses on. "You tell me what you remember that night," she says, "and I'll fill in the blanks, because this is part of what we have to go through."

Telling the story of the crime together is precisely what restorative justice requires victim and offender to "go through." In their *Handbook of Restorative Justice*, authors Dennis Sullivan and Larry Tifft explain that storytelling has the ability to restore emotional well-being for both victim and offender, because the stories we tell ourselves and those we hear from others are what shape our identity and form the bonds of family and friendship.

"I remember being at the front door and I wanted to yell at you," Tim finally says, beginning his fragmented narrative of the night of the rape. "But I didn't remember why I wanted to yell at you, so I didn't. When I called you in and asked you where my food was, in an instant everything got shut off. And rather then, it wasn't like, like I was actually there; it was more like I was watching it on television or something. I remember walking toward the steps and up the steps. I barely remember starting to go down that hallway. The next thing I remember is that I was sitting on the toilet. And your... I had you perform oral sex on me. I remember telling you to stop and jumping in the tub. I don't know how long I was in the tub. Next thing I remember, we were going in the room. You were laying down on the bed, and I remember you asking me not to do it."

"Then why did you?" asks Lyndy, as Tim cries softly. Lyndy is crying too, but she is determined to take full advantage of this meeting with her brother. She picks up the excruciating burden and tells the story where Tim left off.

"That was four thirty in the morning," she says. "That's how long it took because you terrorized me first in the kitchen. You had me up against the back door, a serrated-edge knife against my throat, and you stuck it up near my eye. Then we went upstairs. And I know if I tried to run, you were gonna kill me that night. And then I cried, and you told me to shut up or you were gonna cut my head off."

Together now, the story is told in concert by both, in all its shocking detail. Tim repeats his apology, adding that there's nothing he can do to change the past.

"I'm so sorry. I'm so sorry," he says, still unable, or unwilling, to meet his sister's steady, courageous gaze.

Tim remains engulfed by shame, a constellation of emotions we're told merge wrongdoing with one's sense of self. The shame-infused individual will blame his bad deeds on some defect in himself over which he has no control, but that is rarely the case and certainly not what the victim wishes to hear. Relief will come to the offender and a measure of peace will return to the victim, only if the offender can assume responsibility for his crime, only if he can acknowledge he *could have acted differently, failed to control himself, and is both accountable and regretful for his failure or refusal to stay his hand.* Lyndy, unwilling to accept Tim's expressions of shame and his claims of helplessness, tells him he *can* change the past.

 "You can become a better person than you were that night," she tells him.

The process is almost complete. Offender and victim have met. Together they have made sense of the night of the rape, no matter what terrible sense it made. Lyndy has told her brother how grievous the harm resulting from his actions was. She has held him responsible for it, and challenged him to make a better future—to create some kind of value out of the damage done to her life. Tim has listened; he has spoken the unspeakable, and he has apologized. He has pulled the story out from the darkest place inside of him and laid it out before her. They both know precisely what he's sorry for. He's sorry for her experience, sorry for what that frightful, terrifying, disloyal, violent event cost his sister.

Lyndy heads toward the door by the end of the table where her brother the rapist is sitting, still unable to look her in the eye. She is about to walk by him, but pauses to put her hand lightly on his shoulder. That small gesture, that acknowledgement of the bond that existed before the rape, breaks the dam that has been holding both back for these many years. Lyndy collapses into her brother's arms, and he embraces her. She weeps as he repeats, softly, like a mother would—like a *brother* would—"I'm sorry; I'm so sorry." Astonishingly, Lyndy says she's sorry too. There's something Lyndy has been holding back from her brother, something for which she feels accountable—some way in which she has played a real part in the pain of the crime's aftermath.

"I'm sorry it took so long," she says, her words muffled in his arms.

Two hours later, Lyndy is again in the same room with her brother, summing up her feelings. Before the meeting, she'd told the restorative justice counselors that she could always tell when her brother was lying. Now, she turns to face Tim. "I told them that I would know in my heart that you were really sorry, and that you would be truthful with me. I want you to know that I would not have touched you on the shoulder if I thought that you were lying. The stranger that you became that night on the fourth of November back in 1990 is no longer here. He's gone. And I hope in some way this helps you heal a little bit on the inside and puts you on the right direction."

It is time to go. Tim and Lyndy embrace one more time.

"I love you," says Tim.

"I love you," says Lyndy, and it is over.

Accountability, amends, forgiveness, reconciliation—those are the human activities that can heal victim and community alike, while at the same time restoring the wrongdoer to a law abiding community. The healing and uniting process of restorative justice will never entirely replace trial, conviction, and imprisonment, but it can bring peace to victims like Lyndy, restoring the rent in the social fabric that every crime creates.

W

W is for Women

This is Lorrie. She's a lawyer. She's not, by the way, a "female lawyer" any more than Barack Obama is a male president. Lorrie is a lawyer who is also a woman, and Obama is a president who happens to be—like every President in our country's history—a man.

Lorrie, the lawyer, does have a female *issue*, however. Despite her advanced education, her intelligence, her power as an attorney, her relative degree of prosperity, and her mental toughness, Lorrie is afraid to negotiate. She's not afraid to negotiate for her clients. She does that routinely and effectively. She, like most women, is afraid of negotiating for herself.

Before we get to the *why* of that, I want to tell you a story about Lorrie and negotiation.

Lorrie is a working mother and a trial attorney with two children under five years of age. She had been working for me for six months as a part-time associate in a mid-sized Southern California law firm. She had graduated near the top of her class at UCLA Law School and had previously worked for one of the biggest, best, and most well-respected law firms in the country. Then she had children. Not just one, but three. Lorrie dropped out of practice for several years—years during which her childless colleagues built their books of business, advanced in their law firms, struck out on their own, and honed their practice skills.

Now, Lorrie's youngest was in kindergarten and Lorrie was back. She was one of the best associate attorneys who ever worked for me, and there had been a lot of them. When this story took place, I had been practicing law for twenty-two years. Lorrie was the best senior associate on my trial team. It was December and trial was scheduled for April. The plaintiff, a chain of Southern California pain clinics, was seeking tens of millions of dollars in damages in a lawsuit that had been up to the California Supreme Court and back. My client, a worker's compensation insurance carrier, was accused of conspiring with other insurance companies to drive the pain clinics out of business. It was a big case and an important one. For the previous six months, Lorrie had been working as many—and often more—hours than her full-time peers, juggling her family responsibilities and a crushing workload.

Because Lorrie had worked so hard and so well, I recommended to my law firm's compensation committee that Lorrie receive the full ten thousand dollar year-end bonus being given to all associates who "made their hours" (nineteen hundred billable hours) that year. The compensation committee was unanimous in its approval, so it was surprising when Lorrie stormed into my office, eyes blazing, jaw set.

"What's up?" I asked, looking up from a legal brief that was due to be filed the following day.

"I just got my bonus," Lorrie said through gritted teeth. "And?" I asked.

She threw the check on my desk. "And it's seven thousand dollars."

Now I was angry, too. I picked up the phone, dialed the managing partner, "Bill," and said, "I've got Lorrie here with her seven thousand dollar bonus. Where's the other three grand?"

Here's what happened. The compensation committee had authorized ten thousand dollars, and Bill had it in his budget; however, he wasn't going to open with ten grand. If he could save the firm a little money by negotiating with Lorrie, all the better for the partners, right?

"I expected her to *negotiate*," Bill said in his end-of-discussion tone. "If she'd wanted ten grand, she should have asked for it. I can't change it now. Tell her we'll reward her next year after you and she win the trial."

A month later, Lorrie left the firm.

What happened here is not simply a lesson for management (when *will* they learn?), but a critical teaching moment for all women everywhere.

A significant part of the explanation for the persistence of the thirty-three percent wage and income gap between men and women is the failure of women to negotiate. Here are some statistics:

- By failing to routinely negotiate salaries, women lose more than one million dollars over the course of their careers.

- Although women own forty percent of all businesses in the United States, they receive only 2.3 percent of the available equity capital needed for growth, making women-owned businesses more vulnerable to failure and their employees more vulnerable to job loss.

- Though satisfied with their work performance, women expect to be paid far less than men in identical jobs—four percent less when beginning a career and twenty-three percent less at career peak.

- When asked by researchers to count dots on a square until they felt entitled to earn the four dollars they were being paid to participate in the experiment, women worked twenty-two percent longer and ten percent faster than men, for the same amount of money.

I want you to pay particularly close attention to that last study. Despite the revolution in women's work and career choices over the past thirty years, and despite the vast numbers of women who become lawyers, doctors, engineers, rocket scientists, mathematicians, and nuclear physicists, the thirty-three percent wage gap persists. What if a significant portion of that wage gap could be attributed to women's failure to ask? Women work twenty-two percent longer and ten percent faster before they feel entitled to the same salary as a man. That's thirty-two percent—nearly the entire wage gap.

Women can close that gap tomorrow by learning how to negotiate.

Even better news—women already know how, they just don't think of it as negotiation. As Linda Babcock has written, women are more likely than their male peers to "follow a set of rules or steps" to reach a negotiated agreement. Women are also particularly

> *"The vast changes in the status of women over the last forty years have yet to transform women's opinions about themselves and their right to seek what they want from their workplace, their families, their businesses and their society."*

gifted at seeing the big picture and creating a systematic plan to solve a problem without throwing the entire enterprise out of whack. And, unsurprisingly, women feel more comfortable thinking out loud and sharing experiences when they've been given a problem to solve collaboratively in the best interests of all parties. These are the very same qualities that the best business schools in the country now recommend as the most efficient and effective means of reaching a negotiated resolution for the most intractable problems in business, economics, and politics.

The vast changes in the status of women over the last forty years have yet to transform women's opinions about themselves and their right to seek what they want from their workplace, their families, their businesses, and their society.

We begin by giving ourselves permission to *ask*.

"May we have the table by the window?"

"My son has special needs. I'd like to talk to someone who can tell me what options are available for his early education."

While practicing asking, we begin to research our market value by checking online resources and making local inquiries about pay scales. Then, we ask ourselves how much our work contributes to our employer's bottom line or how much our services contribute to our customers' or clients' financial well-being. We monetize our value according to market metrics rather than simply consulting our "gut" about how much we *need*.

In firm possession of our market value, we make a strategic plan for getting it. We prepare charts, graphs, and power point presentations. We write down our talking points and take the paper with us into our next client meeting or employee evaluation session. We say what we believe we're entitled to and support it with our market research. We're prepared to bargain, starting two or three steps above the number we believe to represent a fair salary or fee. We justify every bargaining move with a reason and ask our negotiation partner to reciprocate when we make concessions. We separate the people from the problem, building trust with our bargaining partner by being candid about our interests, both in the long- and short-term. We ask diagnostic questions meant to reveal our employer's or our customer's own needs, desires, preferences, and priorities, striving to satisfy as many of them as we can, while at the same time suggesting that value is a two way street. In short, we learn to negotiate, and by negotiating, we never let an opportunity to achieve our goals and the dreams of our families pass us by again.

X

X is for Xenophobe

According to the *Merriam-Webster Online Dictionary*, a xenophobe is "unduly fearful of what is foreign and especially of people of foreign origin." He likes to live in a neighborhood where almost everyone talks like him and walks like him. He likes it best when his friends are the same color and nationality. People who are not like him—foreigners—make him uneasy. He doesn't know what they're thinking and what they believe in. They seem dangerous, treacherous, and unworthy.

> *"Whenever the xenophobe spends time with people unlike him (the others), he generally finds that they have far more in common with him than he originally imagined."*

Whenever the xenophobe spends time with people unlike him (the 'others'), he generally finds that they have far more in common with him than he originally imagined. They all want their children to have a good education and access to medical care. If the others don't go to church on Sunday, they go to a temple on Saturday, or they kneel down in prayer facing Mecca five times a day. The others want to be liked and respected; they need privacy and community, and they believe that, with all its faults, twenty-first-century America is a pretty darn good place to call home.

What the xenophobe doesn't know is that he is as foreign, as dangerous, and as frightening to the others as they are to him. He doesn't know, for instance, that he speaks with a foreign accent.

When President Obama appointed a Latino woman, Sonia Sotomayor, to the United States Supreme Court, many people were afraid that she would bring a Latino and female bias to an institution that was supposed to be neutral on matters of race, gender, religion, nationality, and disability. The fact that people who are not xenophobes questioned whether Sotomayor would, for the first time, bring a Latino-biased point of view to the court seemed odd and disconcerting to many women and people of color.

As many people rightly pointed out at the time, no one asks whether a white man will bring his prejudices to the bench. Why? Because white men have no accent. The dominant culture does not think of itself in terms of race. It doesn't have to. The people with power (still primarily white men) do not need to ask themselves thorny questions about their attitudes toward their own race and gender.

I know a little something about how judges think, because my father was a judicial officer on the Los Angeles Superior Court bench for twenty years. Dad and his family were dust-bowl refugees who worked their way down the California coast picking vegetables on other people's farms after their own farm went bust in Nebraska during the Dirty Thirties. Dad, who didn't become a lawyer until he was forty-two years old, and who never attended a single day of college, used to say that there should be dumb politicians to represent the dumb people. He was exaggerating, of course, to make the point that a representative government should represent *all* of the people, and not just a privileged majority.

Was Dad's life-view affected by his humble origins, by his struggle to overcome an incomplete high school education, by a culture of poverty, and by the burdens of his gender in a mid-century America that assumed only men were obliged to work? You bet it was.

Did anyone ask whether Dad was going to bring a white, male, depression-era bias to the Bench? No. Did he? Of course he did. Still, Dad leaned as far away from his mid-twentieth-century white male privilege as he could—drafting marital agreements for gay clients from the late 1960s until he went on the bench, voting against his economic self-interest in every presidential election (proudly asserting that he paid more in federal income tax than he used to make annually), and supporting all civil rights movements—African-American, Chicano (the term of that day), women, and gays.

Dad was a good guy, aware of his biases and willing to push against them. It is not, however, possible for any of us to be without bias. An article in the *Cornell Law Review*, "Blinking on the Bench: How Judges Decide Cases," demonstrates the bias of influence. In that study, psychologists tested a negotiation theory known as anchoring. When making monetary estimates in an atmosphere of uncertainty, people commonly rely on the initial estimate given to them. This first estimate provides a starting point for the generation of a judgment that exerts a stronger influence than subsequent pieces of information. Not only do these initial numbers influence negotiators, they've been found to influence judicial decision-makers. The researchers demonstrated that a ten million dollar demand made at a pre-hearing settlement conference anchored judges' assessments of the appropriate amount of damages to award. Judges in a control group awarded the party seeking damages between seven hundred thousand and eight hundred thousand dollars, while judges in the anchor group awarded a much larger number—between one and 2.2 million dollars.

Studies such as this show that anchors have a powerful influence on judgments. This is what we litigators and trial attorneys do for a living. We try to anchor judges. We spin the facts and expand the outer reaches of the law in a way that helps our clients. We read judicial profiles to know as much we can about a judge—his or her background, politics, charities, family life, and prior decisions—so that we can speak his or her language. No one knows better than litigators and trial lawyers the importance of an individual judge's background, ethnicity, political affiliations, and probable bias.

So back we come to Justice Sotomayor. Is she bringing to the Supreme Court a viewpoint never before represented there? Yes, she is. Is that a problem in a society as diverse as ours is? Not really. A democracy will always evolve in the direction of enfranchisement for all of its citizens. As the dictionary tells us, enfranchisement's primary and commonly understood definition is the act of endowing a country's inhabitants with the rights of citizenship. Those rights include not only the right to vote—a right originally reserved only to white men who owned property—but also the right to reap the benefits and bear the burdens of the political community we inhabit.

In America, the twentieth century was a great era of enfranchisement. Women earned the right to vote in 1920. African-Americans earned the right to send their children to the same public schools their white neighbors in 1954. Women earned the right to share in public monies devoted to sports in 1972. And in some American states, at the turn of the twenty-first century, gay, lesbian, and bisexual citizens earned the right to marry.

What can the enfranchisement of the others do for the xenophobe? If he can set aside his fear, it can widen the circle of people who are "us" and narrow the field of people who are "them." And once that happens, a woman whose ancestors were American slaves can become America's First Lady beside a man whose father was African and whose mother was white.

As we learned in the chapter "K is for Kin," when we increase the number of people we consider to be included in our family, we tend to start playing together in a spirit of cooperation. And as evolution has taught us, it is the cooperative, not the combative, community that survives.

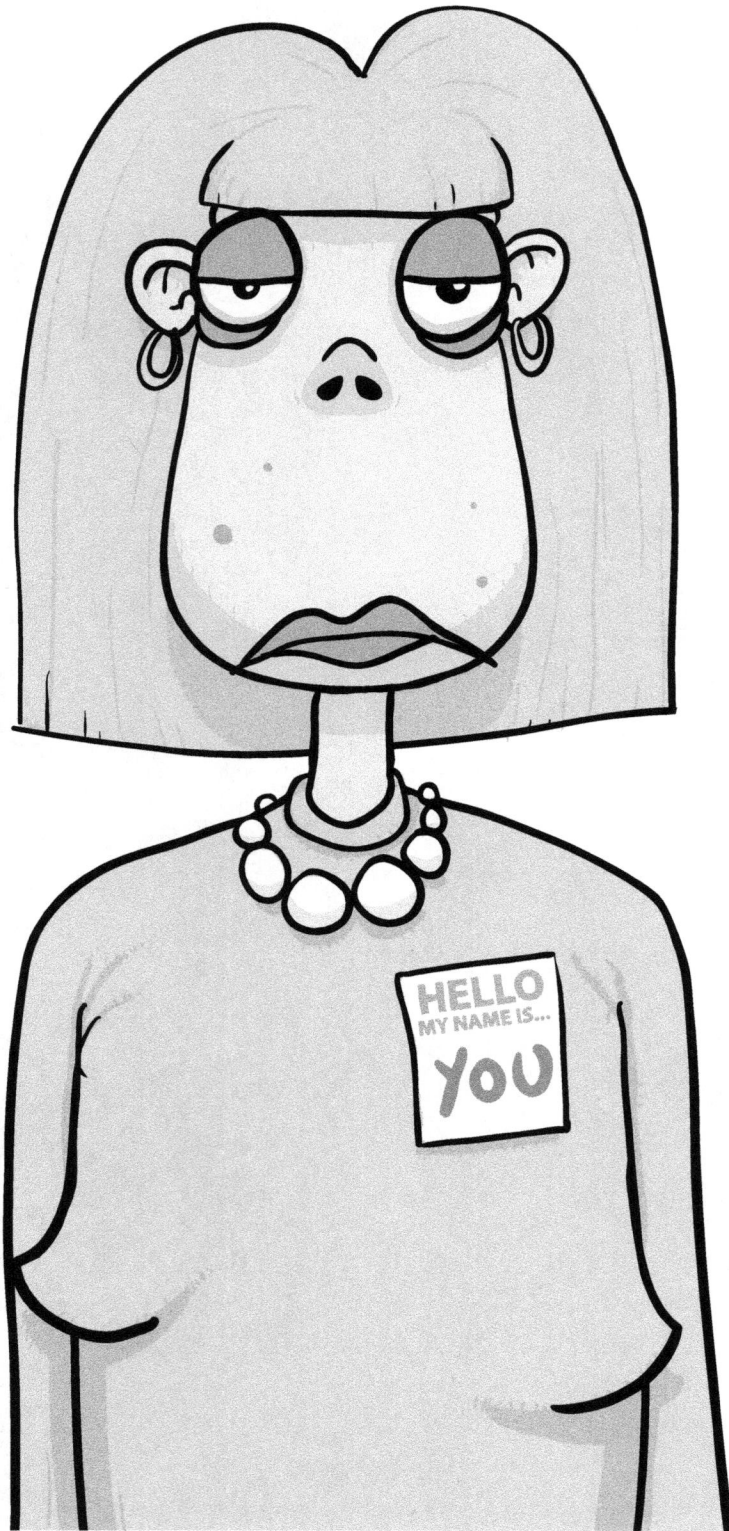

Y

Y is for You

You.

Yes—*you!*

If you leave the resolution of conflict in the hands of the other guy, what do you usually get for it? Continued conflict. Sometimes the conflict is suppressed or avoided, but that doesn't mean it isn't there, creating anxiety and resentment, subtly undermining the best of relationships, or one day bursting into rage, physical violence, or all out war. If we leave the resolution of conflict to the other guy, we will never be in possession of our own separate peace.

Joseph Campell, that famous master of myth and comparative religions, observed of all journeys to enlightenment that we enter the forest at the darkest point where there is no path. If we find and follow someone else's way, we will not realize our own unique potential. So here is where we begin—where each of us is currently residing—in a cottage by the beach or apartment in the city. We are each standing at the edge of our own forest where it is darkest and most resistant to our entry.

Think of yourself as a playing piece on a Monopoly board. Pick the Scotty Dog or the Top Hat, the Thimble or the Race Car. If you're standing on "Go," but believe yourself to already be on Park Place, your roll of the dice will not avail you. You can only move forward if you know you're on "Go."

That's what this book is calculated to do—to put us on conflict "go" again. Those of us who've reached the light of Utility Company's square may not have been able to translate spiritual lessons learned to filling the Community Chest, or purchasing a modest dwelling on St. James Place. We're paying luxury taxes without seeing the benefit we thought we'd derive from the material goods on which taxes continue to accrue. Some of us have landed in jail. Perhaps not the jail of civic authority, but prison nonetheless —unsatisfying jobs, relationships gone awry, family obligations that entrap us and make us feel guilty for feeling confined, or internal beliefs that keep us from moving over the square of Chance.

> *"When we begin to examine conflict from our own part in its creation, we can freely choose whether we wish to avoid or suppress it, resolve it, move past or transcend it, or use it as an opportunity to transform our experience of the "other" in our lives."*

When we begin to examine conflict from our own part in its creation, we can freely choose whether we wish to avoid or suppress it, resolve it, move past or transcend it, or use it as an opportunity to transform our experience of the "other" in our lives. The most important negotiation any of us can conduct is the bargaining we do with ourselves. Where have we been selfish or unkind? In what ways are we being intolerant of another? When are we bullying and manipulating, attempting to coerce someone else to do our bidding or agree with our values? Once we are clear about our own weaknesses and strengths, we can afford to set aside our fears of disclosure long enough to ask our spouses, children, neighbors, and co-workers how we might all might be of mutual service to one another to achieve the greatest number of our interests simultaneously or one after the other. If we are "mindful," the potential for transformation is present. As Dr. Kenneth Cloke has written,

> *Mindfulness is the capacity to be present and aware of what is happening inside you while at the same time developing awareness of what is happening inside others. It includes the experience of relationships as malleable and subject to transformation at any moment. A negotiator exercising mindfulness practices a type of concentration that gives rise to insight and creative intervention techniques. Whenever we allow ourselves to hear at a deep level what the other person is saying, credit it, discover its meaning, and give ourselves permission to present that meaning in the form of questions, we are using mindfulness to inform the negotiation process.*

Use the insights you have gained from reading this book as if you were standing at the edge of negotiation's forest. You, and we, will together encounter friends, enemies, guides, fears, failures, and successes, until we finally find the wings to fly to a destination we never knew was possible to reach.

Z

Z is for Zen Master

I have saved the best conflict resolution news for the final chapter. Conflict is your Zen master.

"What the heck is a Zen master?" you ask, "and what possible use could he be in resolving my argument with my teenage daughter, my next-door neighbor, my co-worker, landlord, tenant, parent, sibling, or mother-in-law?"

A Zen master is a Buddhist teacher who helps students achieve enlightenment. Zen masters encourage the abandonment of materialism and rational thought, giving students intellectually baffling puzzles called *koans* upon which to mediate. These koans are not puzzles to be resolved rationally like Sudoku or crosswords. Koans are deliberately irrational or paradoxical statements designed to wake students up to the metaphysical and spiritual truths that lurk behind the façade of the material world.

In the *ABCs of Conflict Resolution,* conflict is your Zen master, and the particular dispute in which you are engaged is the koan by which you can achieve enlightenment.

Let's start with the way in which we traditionally think of conflict—as a negative state of human relations best avoided. Over newspapers and cereal, we do not say to our morning companion, "Hey, did you see the front page? Hostilities have broken out again in Lebanon. Isn't that great?"

Neither do we respond with surprise when we read that another bomb has exploded in downtown Tel Aviv.

"They're at it again," we say with genuine dismay. "It's probably Hamas. Religion causes all of the world's troubles. It will never change."

We shake our heads, sigh, and reach for the orange juice. "Why can't these people just get along?"

When thinking about conflicts in which other people are engaged, it's relatively easy to prescribe remedies. The conflict avoidant might recommend building walls between hostile countries to decrease or avoid armed conflict. That's precisely what Israel has been doing on its borders for many years and what many Americans wish the United States would do on its border with Mexico.

Those who respond to conflict with violence might echo the view of U.S. Air Force General Curtis LeMay, who suggested in 1968 that America should have bombed its enemy, North Vietnam, back into the Stone Age. Those who prefer to suppress conflict tend to stifle free speech, as China continues to do. Those who seek a final, if not necessarily happy, resolution to conflict tend to appeal to higher authorities—judges, legislators, and the like—to adopt laws favoring their solutions and to oppose the creation of laws or decisions with which they disagree.

Finality of decision is one of the great achievements of the justice system. As generations of law students have learned, the Supreme Court is not final because it is right, it is right because it is final. Even if we disagree with a final resolution of conflict, we are nevertheless able to plan our future actions and negotiate our relationships based upon the rules of conduct that we agree govern us all.

Dr. Kenneth Cloke tells us that every conflict "occurs at the intersection, or crossroads, between problems we need to solve in order to grow and skills we do not yet possess. With each level of growth and development, we experience fresh conflicts and transcend old ones that we not only successfully resolve, but develop the skills to move beyond."

Let's take marriage, or long-term relationships of any kind. Whenever I complain about a conflict with my husband, my friend the Buddhist reminds me that my husband is my Zen master. Her reminder focuses my attention back on me and what I have to learn from the dispute I'm having with my husband. The two of us are like the couple in Anne Tyler's novel, *The Accidental Tourist*. We sometimes feel like rivals competing for the "better housekeeper" award. Should I win the prize for insight and understanding even though I am haphazard and mercurial in my habits? Or should the blue ribbon be awarded to my husband who is methodical and steady? When we first met, he loved my spontaneity and I, his dependable nature. Now his steadiness irritates me and my disorganization angers him.

> *"When I change in a fundamental way, the people in my life inevitably change in relation to my change. "*

This intractable meta dispute—the dispute on which all others are based—evaporates when I realize it has something to teach me about my own character and presents a challenge against which that character could possibly develop. The second step is to solve the immediate problem. "If only you'd put your car keys in the same place every time," my husband says for the umpteenth time, "you wouldn't have to spend twenty minutes searching for them." I could choose to shift the argument to my home court ("you are too controlling"), or take the lesson that a little advance planning might ease, rather than burden my busy day.

Here's the transformative part. When I change in a fundamental way, the people in my life inevitably change in relation to my change. Once my husband and I resolve the order-versus-chaos problem, he will have to find another player with whom to play this game or give it up altogether. If his desire is truly to help me lead a more orderly life rather than "trying to control me," the two of us can move on to greater, more interesting challenges than this one, on which we have been stuck for years. The same is true for relations between workers, members of extended families, red states and blue, and Americans against the rest of the world. If we were finally able to resolve our differences over, say, the separation of church and state, we could free up our energy to address other pressing problems, like poverty and intolerance, the environment and health care, and full employment for anyone with the desire to work as a contributing member of the society.

Conflict among human societies has caused incalculable loss and suffering. It is also the way in which people have finally stood up for human rights, self-governance, peaceful dispute resolution, independence, and tolerance of differences. If we encounter conflict with courage and self-reflection, it can and will lead us, and those who surround us, to greater freedom and authenticity, to greater self-reliance, acceptance, accountability, forgiveness, and at long last, a far more peaceful world.

www.ingramcontent.com/pod-product-compliance
Lightning Source LLC
Chambersburg PA
CBHW051215200326
41519CB00025B/7118